A FAN'S LIFE

A FAN'S LIFE

THE AGONY OF VICTORY AND
THE THRILL OF DEFEAT

PAUL CAMPOS

The University of Chicago Press   CHICAGO AND LONDON

The University of Chicago Press, Chicago 60637
© 2022 by Paul F. Campos
All rights reserved. No part of this book may be used or reproduced in any
manner whatsoever without written permission, except in the case of brief
quotations in critical articles and reviews. For more information, contact the
University of Chicago Press, 1427 E. 60th St., Chicago, IL 60637.
Published 2022
Printed in the United States of America

31 30 29 28 27 26 25 24 23 22   1 2 3 4 5

ISBN-13: 978-0-226-82348-5 (paper)
ISBN-13: 978-0-226-82349-2 (e-book)
DOI: https://doi.org/10.7208/chicago/9780226823492.001.0001

Library of Congress Cataloging-in-Publication Data

Names: Campos, Paul F., author.
Title: A fan's life : the agony of victory and the thrill of defeat / Paul Campos.
Description: Chicago ; London : The University of Chicago Press, 2022.
Identifiers: LCCN 2022011152 | ISBN 9780226823485 (paperback) |
ISBN 9780226823492 (e-book)
Subjects: LCSH: Sports spectators—Psychology. | Fans (Persons)—Psychology. |
Sports—Social aspects—United States. | Sports—Political aspects—United States.
Classification: LCC GV715.C35 2022 | DDC 306.4/830973—dc23/eng/20220408
LC record available at https://lccn.loc.gov/2022011152

♾ This paper meets the requirements of ANSI/NISO Z39.48-1992
(Permanence of Paper).

FOR WILLIAM IAN MILLER

CONTENTS

FIVE DAYS
IN MARCH

The first sign that something big was about to happen came on Sunday night, March 8. The ATP and WTA tours—the top levels of men's and women's professional tennis—announced that the BNP Paribas Open, scheduled to start the next day in Indian Wells, California, was canceled.

Indian Wells is the second-most prestigious tennis tournament held in the United States every year, trailing only the US Open. That it had been canceled at the last minute because of the COVID-19 epidemic sent a shudder through the sports world. Over the next week, the Indian Wells cancellation would prove to be a harbinger of unprecedented events in that world.

On Wednesday, March 11, NBA star Rudy Gobert received a positive test result for COVID-19. His team's game was canceled immediately, just before the tipoff, and his teammates were quarantined in their locker room for several hours. Later that evening the NBA announced it was suspending its season indefinitely. The next day, Major League Baseball, the National Hockey League, and Major League Soccer followed suit.

Over the course of Thursday and Friday, all the major European soccer leagues suspended their seasons. The Champions League—roughly the Super Bowl of world club soccer—was also suspended. The PGA—host of the world's top golf tour—suspended play on Friday.

Within five days, essentially all the world's major sporting leagues and tours had shut down. As the fields were emptied and the stands went silent, the multibillion-dollar sports broadcasting and journalism world found itself with nothing to broadcast and only one story to cover.

This radical disruption of the previously dependable rhythms of the sports calendar was perhaps the earliest and most striking sign of the havoc the COVID-19 pandemic would wreak on the entire world. In retrospect the foresight of the major North American sports leagues was remarkable. They shut down before any government had issued stay-at-home orders, and when the total death toll from the virus in the United States was still less than fifty people.

Without that calendar, I became increasingly unmoored in time: like a druid without his monolith, I often lost track of what day of the week or even what month it was. Those of us not bound by the rhythms of agriculture have come to depend on all sorts of artificial markers of the passage of time, sports seasons key among them for many.

This book was written in the shadow of the COVID-19 pandemic. When the games all went away, the significance of the countless hours I had spent over my half century as a sports fan came abruptly into sharper focus. Why do we deeply engaged fans choose to live our lives in this way? That suddenly seemed like a question worth asking.

Over my head, I see the bronze butterfly,
Asleep on the black trunk,
Blowing like a leaf in green shadow.
Down the ravine behind the empty house,
The cowbells follow one another
Into the distances of the afternoon.
To my right,
In a field of sunlight between two pines,
The droppings of last year's horses
Blaze up into golden stones.
I lean back, as the evening darkens and comes on.
A chicken hawk floats over, looking for home.
I have wasted my life.

"LYING IN A HAMMOCK AT WILLIAM DUFFY'S
FARM IN PINE ISLAND, MINNESOTA"
JAMES WRIGHT

THEY DIDN'T LISTEN TO JESUS EITHER

The first faint shiver of this book came to me on New Year's Day 1997. I was surfing the Internet with the vague idea of finding someone to talk with about the University of Michigan's football team, which had just lost its bowl game to Alabama in a particularly absurd and excruciating manner. The Wolverines had been driving deep in Alabama territory in the fourth quarter. They—we—had the lead and were on the verge of scoring an apparent game-clinching touchdown when quarterback Brian Griese tried to get rid of the ball as he was being hit by a blitzing defensive back. The resulting pass looked like something a small child would throw in a backyard game of catch; the ball fluttered forward for about 5 yards before landing in the arms of an Alabama linebacker, who immediately raced 88 yards downfield for the game-winning score.

I had just discovered the cyberworld, so I didn't really know where to look for such a conversation. I don't recall what search engine I used—Google didn't exist yet—but I stumbled onto a message board dedicated to discussing University of Michigan sports, mainly football.

The very first post I read was an agonized jeremiad from "Brent" that went into great detail about how this game illustrated, as he had been pointing out at length for two seasons now, that the hiring of Lloyd Carr as Michigan's head coach had been an unmitigated disaster. Indeed, only the most deluded of optimists could possibly still believe that things could get appreciably better as long as Carr remained in that position. On the other hand, Brent noted, the rejection of his prophecy by the board's "sunshine blowers" was only to be expected. After all, the Gospels recorded how, in biblical times, "they didn't listen to Jesus either," Brent reminded them—or rather, us—as I read on in rapt fascination. (It would be uncharitable to point out that one year later to the day Michigan would win the national championship.)

"Now in no way am I comparing myself to Jesus Christ," Brent hastened to add. Somehow this caveat was lost on the rest of the board, which, already roiled in the kind of bitter arguments and recriminations that I soon learned were the inevitable products of any Michigan loss, unleashed a furious barrage of scorn and sarcasm against the self-styled prophet.

Here, I realized, are my people. And, nearly a quarter century later, I'm still there.

This book is, among other things, a memoir of being a deeply engaged sports fan in the age of the Internet. I have been a sports fan for almost exactly fifty years—I discovered team sports at the age of ten, after being largely oblivious to them until that point—and I have spent almost exactly half of that time following sports on the Internet. And fandom is ultimately about one's memories of being a fan, which is to say that nostalgia is its basic fuel.

Yet at this particular moment in American life, indulging in nostalgia has become fraught in all sorts of ways. This book explores how the psychological experience of fandom is related to the longing for an idealized past fueling the wave of political reaction that has swept over the country in recent years.

The Internet has changed—and come to dominate—life in countless ways, but it is especially striking how it has created a complex world of communities: in particular communities that allow people with an especially passionate interest in a subject to find one another, to share and often intensify that passion to the point of obsession and fanaticism—the concept from which we get "fan." This should be a source of happiness—especially if you believe the economic premise that consumers rationally try to maximize their enjoyment of different kinds of leisure or entertainment.

Yet being a fan of anything or anyone, especially in this mediated context, tends to make us deeply unhappy. Fandom, fundamentally, isn't about happiness; indeed, it is about unhappiness—specifically, the kind of communal unhappiness of people who choose to be unhappy together rather than to suffer alone.

People who hate sports in general and sports fandom in particular sometimes mock such passions with the word "sportsball," signaling disdain for pointless and irrational allegiances to various teams. Yet there's an approximately 83 percent chance, I'd wager, that anyone who uses the word "sportsball" has gotten into furious arguments about whether Han Solo shot first in the bar scene in *Star Wars* and/or has actually written fan fiction of some kind—which is to say, fandom isn't limited to sports. Fandom is ultimately egalitarian: for instance, someone who reads the works of Michel Foucault and someone who pays $9.99 a month for access to the World Wrestling Entertainment Network can both be fanatically devoted to worshipping or despising the Dallas Cowboys. They can sometimes even be the same person.

The Internet, of course, fuels obsession. And obsession, too, ranges far beyond sports. In cyberspace, the mental world of the deeply engaged sports fan—captured concisely by novelist and fanatical Arsenal football club supporter Nick Hornby thus: "For alarmingly large chunks of an average day, I am a moron"—can easily migrate into many other realms, especially politics. The essence of fandom, in fact, is partisanship, and tribalism and schadenfreude are the characteristic mental states of our time; both make otherwise intelligent people stupid and stupid people even stupider.

For a football team to elicit fandom is usually fairly benign; for a political movement or leader to do so is definitely not. Yet in American culture, the distinction between sports and politics is being blurred increasingly, by people seeking to profit from that blurring. The blurring has a pronounced and not arbitrary ideological tilt. Being drunk on ethno-nationalism, it turns out, is very similar to being drunk on rooting for your favorite team, or being drunk, period. In 2012 researchers went into a bar and asked questions of eighty-five drinkers. As people got drunker, their answers became more politically conservative. The authors' conclusion? "Because alcohol limits cognitive capacity and leaves automatic thinking largely intact, these data are consistent with our claim that low-effort thinking promotes political conservatism."

Ethno-nationalism, in particular, reduces what social scientists refer to as "cognitive load" by transferring the crude psychological allegiances sports fans have for their teams to a racialized vision of the nation-state. Deeply engaged fandom by its nature also limits cognitive capacity and leaves automatic thinking largely intact, which is why demagogues do everything possible to make their political rallies indistinguishable from a pep rally before the Big Game. (Flaubert: "To be stupid, selfish, and have good health are three requirements for happiness, though if stupidity is lacking, all is lost.")

Yet deeply engaged fandom can be a good thing, too. When it stays in the world of sports, it can promote the kind of community that is otherwise lost in our increasingly atomized society. More than twenty years ago, in his book *Bowling Alone*, the sociologist Robert Putnam used the decline of bowling leagues as both an example of and a metaphor for the decline of traditional social networks. Things haven't gotten better since then. But the world of sports message boards can be a kind of antidote to surfing the Internet alone. The friendships people develop there are very real—especially, perhaps, for middle-aged and older men, who often find themselves isolated in a society where so many institutions (such as fraternal lodges, labor unions, and religious organizations) that once created and sustained communities have deteriorated or disappeared. Sports in general, and fandom in particular, can serve as windows not only into the microsocieties they create, but into society as a whole—into the broader worlds of politics, economics, and culture. (Note that this book offers an array of perspectives on fandom, not a lawyerly brief for or against it.)

A few years before that 1997 Michigan–Alabama game, I saw the Italian film *Bread and Chocolate*. The hero, a southern Italian, has emigrated to Switzerland as a lowly "guest worker." Surrounded by idyllic landscapes and obnoxiously beautiful people, he becomes disgusted with the dirt and chaos and poverty of his homeland. He decides to pass as Swiss, dyes his hair blond, adopts the local language and customs, and generally does everything he can to blend in.

The film's climatic scene takes place in a bar, where he is watching the Italian national soccer team play Switzerland. He is of course surrounded by Swiss fans, who are raucously supporting their team while mocking and denigrating the Italian side. He becomes increasingly agitated, until suddenly Italy scores. The bar falls dead silent. He looks around at his compatriots, and, after a moment, leaps to his feet and screams, his voice almost strangled with passion: "Goal! Gooaal! Gooooaaal!" That passion is mine too.

FANDOM IS FOLLY

In the 1970s, a pair of Israeli psychologists started exploring some curious results that kept showing up in their experiments. Classical economic theory assumes that people—or at least a mythical "rational economic actor"—will treat the prospect of either winning something or losing it in the same way. But Daniel Kahneman and Amos Tversky discovered this wasn't true: the large majority of people were not "rational," in this sense. They devised a series of ingenious tests illustrating that most people hate to lose much more than they like to win.

Here is one of them: Suppose you are given $1,000. Then you are given a choice: you can either be given $500 more or flip a coin. If you win the coin flip, you win an additional $1,000. But if you lose it, you win nothing additional and are left with $1,000.

If you neither get extra pleasure from the mere act of gambling nor extra pain from regret and you are a "rational actor," you will be indifferent to these two options, which are, statistically speaking, equivalent. But the large majority of people are not, in fact, indifferent: roughly seven out of ten people choose the sure thing rather than the coin flip.

One plausible explanation for this might be that most people are risk averse: that is, they tend to value a sure thing over a gamble, even one of an equivalent value. Kahneman and Tversky tested that hypothesis by tweaking the experiment. This time, subjects were told they were being given $2,000 to begin with. Then they had to decide to either give back $500 or flip a coin and, if they lost, give back $1,000. Statistically speaking, these two experiments are identical: people who prefer a sure thing will collect their $1,500, while risk-seeking people will gamble on ending up with either $2,000 or $1,000.

If the explanation for the large majority choosing the sure thing in the first experiment is risk aversion, then you would expect that an equally large majority would choose to give back $500 in the second scenario. But Kahneman and Tversky reported something startling: the results of their two experiments were not only inconsistent—they were essentially reversed! When the sure thing required giving money back, the large majority of subjects preferred to gamble, rather than taking the sure thing. Kahneman and Tversky dubbed their explanation for this type of apparently contradictory behavior "prospect theory."

At the core of prospect theory is the insight that most people are risk averse when considering potential gains—or more precisely, when considering what they frame in their minds as potential gains—and risk-seeking when considering what they think of as potential losses. In other words, most of us hate losing a lot more than we like winning. As Kahneman and Tversky put it, most of us are not risk averse but rather "loss averse."

Kahneman's and Tversky's revolutionary work became the basis of what is now known as behavioral economics. (Kahneman was awarded the Nobel Prize for economics in 2002, a few years after his colleague's death.) Behavioral economics challenges the assumption that people are rational, at least in the traditional economic sense. It does so by looking at how people actually behave.

Both classical and behavioral economics are, however, still based on the idea that people seek to, in the jargon of the trade, "maximize their utility." Economists assume we pursue things we want while avoiding things we dislike. That assumption seems true practically by definition. Yet it becomes problematic when we do something as simple as peruse an Internet sports message board, where passionate fans of a particular team gather to share, in more or less real time, the experience of watching their favorite team compete.

On the Michigan board, the emotion that usually dominates the messages posted during any game in which Michigan has not yet secured victory is abject misery. Anger, disgust, frustration, and despair will also be on display, via the most florid and profane vocabulary. This does not—if we assume people pursue pleasure or happiness and flee from their opposites—seem to make much sense. After all, we passionate fans are not at that moment engaged in labor, which is understood to involve tolerating a certain amount of unpleasantness in exchange for money, but rather in "consumption," which are the activities we enjoy enough to prefer them to spending that time making yet more money.

I have worked in various jobs over the past thirty-five years. I've sometimes been among a lot of unhappy employees, including myself. But I've never been in a work environment in which the typical worker came within a country mile of achieving the level of unhappiness experienced by the typical board poster—again, including myself—during the typical Michigan game. I suspect that in such a workplace, everyone would quit their jobs by the end of the day, if not before lunch.

Yet, mysteriously enough, this is what we choose to do for "fun." No one, other than our own hopelessly addicted selves, subjects us to this profound misery, which only grows for a big game, and most especially for The Game itself. The Game, reverently capitalized, is the annual end-of-season contest between Michigan and Ohio State.

Fandom, it would seem, is folly, at least from the perspective of classical economics. Yet it is even more incomprehensible when we consider the insights of behavioral economics. If we hate to lose much more than we like to win (and we on the board certainly do), and if sports are zero-sum—that is, if every victory for someone is by ruthless logical necessity a loss for someone else—then being a deeply engaged fan, bedeviled by inevitable losing, is practically a species of madness.

Why do people allow something that so often makes them profoundly miserable to become one of the ruling passions of their lives? If I had a dollar for every time I've heard a board denizen claim that this is it, he's quitting, this is absurd, he's finally had enough, thank

God he'll now have something better to do with his autumn Saturdays, and so on and so forth, I would be able to torture myself inside a luxury box (annual rent $80,000 or more, tickets not included) at the Big House itself, a.k.a. Michigan Stadium, instead of sweltering or shivering in the—relatively—cheap seats, or more often in the climate-controlled comfort of my living room, while I curse at the TV and my wife asks what's wrong with me.

It's a good question. What is wrong with me or, more interestingly, with all of us, since our affliction is widespread enough to support various multibillion-dollar industries?

At this point, an anthropologist observing this particular tribe would make some distinctions. For one, not everyone watching a game, whether in person or via media, is a fan in the sense I've been using the term. Any sporting event will feature a spectrum of spectators that runs from the most casual consumption to the deepest emotional engagement. That spectrum can be sorted into three broad categories.

The first category of spectators has little or often literally no interest in the outcome of the contest. These people are spectating for all sorts of reasons, which run from providing companionship to someone who actually cares about the outcome to enjoying the event as sheer spectacle to engaging in a classic form of conspicuous consumption. In recent years I've been struck by how often people in the most expensive seats—courtside at an NBA game, center court at a major tennis tournament—are paying no attention whatsoever to the action and seem permanently on their smartphones, even as they occupy $2,000 seats that a truly passionate fan would do almost anything to acquire. As the cost of attendance at big events skyrockets ever-upward in the new gilded age, that type of nonspectating spectator becomes both increasingly conspicuous and increasingly deplorable.

These people are not really fans: they are only spectators. But fans in one context can be spectators in another. I've been to plenty of sporting events and watched countless numbers on TV in which I never developed even the most tenuous interest in the outcome. For example, I've been to major league baseball games on beautiful late summer days, between teams that I've never followed even casually and who are already out of postseason contention and are therefore playing a "meaningless game"—although as we shall see there are actually no meaningless games. This is one of life's enjoyable experiences: a relaxing afternoon at the ballpark. But it is not really a part of the world of genuine fandom, even by vicarious extension.

Nonfans play an important role in the economy of big-money sports—for one thing, it's difficult to fill a huge stadium without them—but they are irrelevant to the world of passion, pain, and all-too-occasional ecstasy that make up a fan's life.

The second category, casual fans, on the other hand, are extremely relevant to that life, since almost all fans are casual fans almost all the time. A casual fan is someone who cares in some sense about the outcome of a contest yet remains less than fully committed to an emotional investment in it. The casual fan is someone who, crucially, has experienced the deep engagement of genuine fandom, but who is not experiencing it now, except perhaps by a kind of proxy. Casual fans are engaged to the extent they are, only because they have been deeply engaged in other contexts. I watch an enormous amount of sports of all kinds, and for the overwhelming majority of that time, I am a casual fan.

For instance, when I watched the seventh game of the 2016 World Series between the Chicago Cubs and the Cleveland Indians, I had a slight rooting preference for the Cubs, but my dominant emotion was a very powerful sense of how terrifyingly engrossing every pitch, especially in the late stages, must have been for deeply engaged fans. (When Rajai Davis hit a three-run homer to tie the score in the bottom of the eighth inning, I had the disorienting sensation of feeling simultaneously a distant echo of both the sudden agony of Cubs fans and the short-lived ecstasy of their Cleveland counterparts.)

One of the striking aspects of being, at least occasionally, a deeply engaged fan is that it makes it easy to enjoy this kind of vicarious engagement: to be what in soccer jargon is referred to as a "neutral"—someone whose primary interest is in seeing a good game but who nevertheless will almost inevitably develop some sort of rooting interest, if only out of psychological habit. The strength of that habit is attested to by such phenomena as how fans at a ballpark will, during a break between innings, root for a particular outcome of an electronic "race" between three different-colored cars projected on the scoreboard, even though literally nothing turns on this completely imaginary competition.

This sort of shallow engagement is surely the most common psychological state of sports fans, and it is crucial to the economic structure of the whole enterprise; again, stadiums have a lot of seats to fill. But that shallow engagement is ultimately nothing but a faint echo of the deep engagement that is the real key to the whole thing. We settle for shallow engagement because it is a pleasant and painless reminder of something rarely pleasant and never painless: our profound, and profoundly strange, emotional investment in the relative handful of contests we really care about.

And here we encounter the central paradox: sports are a form of entertainment, but deep engagement, which makes the entire sports branch of the entertainment industrial complex viable, is not about entertainment at all: it is about suffering.

That entertainment and genuine fandom have almost nothing to do with each other is captured perfectly in a vignette from *Fever Pitch*, Nick Hornby's classic memoir of life as a supporter of the Arsenal soccer club. After a particularly dull match, in which the opposing manager was criticized by journalists for his negative tactics—meaning those adopted with no consideration whatever for the aesthetic value of a match that neutrals might enjoy watching—the manager snarled, "If you want entertainment, go and watch clowns."

The high-brow sporting press naturally had a field day with this comment. Imagine the director of a big-budget Hollywood extravaganza responding to critics who claimed the movie was boring not by denying the charge but by asserting that whether or not a movie was boring was irrelevant to evaluating it! Yet Hornby concludes that the manager was right: "Complaining about boring football is a little like complaining about the sad ending of *King Lear*: it misses the point somehow." The deeply engaged fan, Hornby notes, goes to games for lots of reasons, but entertainment isn't one of them.

For the genuine fan, deep engagement is a qualitatively different experience than casual fandom. The shallow engagement of the latter is, in fact, a search for mere entertainment, while the deeply engaged seek not entertainment but the catharsis that comes from a community bound together by, above all, the experience of shared suffering.

Deeply engaged fans know what it is to wake up, after a night of uneasy dreams, to a sensation of nausea and dread, as we contemplate the many hours before kickoff. We know what it is to relive again and again, through the insidious power of involuntary memory, the dropped interception that surely would have won that game five or fifteen or forty years ago. We know what it is to keep, among many, many other things, obsessive mental catalogs of final scores, starting lineups, nonsensical coaching decisions, and horrible officiating blunders—always going against our team, needless to say. Complaining about officiating—as well as complaining about fans who complain about officiating—are constitutive aspects of deep engagement. If you cannot recall off the top of your head a dozen occasions when your team was well and truly screwed by the refs, you are not a deeply engaged fan.

These and countless other forms of arcana pile up in a kind of enormous mental garbage dump—the cognitive flotsam and jetsam of genuine fandom. For example, my friend Rich, an otherwise completely normal, charismatic, and professionally successful Michigan graduate, with whom I have attended many a game, can name the precise starting times of games Michigan played in the NCAA basketball tournament several decades ago. He could also write a PhD dissertation on the most subtle changes to Michigan's football uniform over the past five decades. But what we seem to remember best are the worst losses, whose details we regularly recount with each other in a kind of masochistic ritual that marks our membership in this least exclusive of clubs.

For fans, deep engagement is ultimately about suffering. Why do we suffer? To prove we're serious, that we're alive, that we care, that all this expenditure of time and money and mental and emotional energy is for something that does matter in some nonpathological way. Meanwhile, as time goes on, we find increasingly that the losses are pure agony, while victory brings only temporary relief from ever more certain future suffering. In many ways, genuine fandom resembles the psychological experience of a drug addict, who eventually loses the ability to extract real pleasure from the drug but nevertheless needs to keep taking it, if only to escape an unbearable craving.

On one level, of course, all of this is ridiculous and deplorable. Why should grown men, most of them highly educated, successful, and deeply engaged by far more respectable passions—politics, economics, climate change, their hopes and dreams for their children, etc.—give themselves over so wholly, so excessively, to this apparently trivial pursuit? And they are men: a striking feature of the Michigan board is that it seems to be an almost exclusively male space. The extent to which, and the reasons why, obsessive fandom, especially as it manifests itself in venues such as traditional Internet message boards, is a disproportionately male phenomenon are complex and fraught topics. Obviously many individual women are obsessive fans, whether of sports teams or of any of the many other objects of devotion that lend themselves to this type of obsession. Yet in my experience the vast majority of obsessive fans tend to be men. (I make no claim for the universality of my experience in this regard.)

In any event, I'm painfully aware of how absurd devoted fandom looks from the outside, since I'm often on the outside myself—a casual fan at best. When I watch a YouTube video of a fan of the famous Argentine soccer club River Plate witnessing his team suffer the ultimate indignity of relegation to a lower division as he screams the most astonishing Spanish obscenities at the television over and over again (his wife's voice in the background, deploring his evident insanity), I recognize how indefensible fandom—my own fandom—really is.

Yet although sports fandom in particular may be folly, it is, ultimately, not so different from the many other constitutive passions that make us who we are. After all, romantic love is absurd when seen from the outside, as is a passion for the early films of Dario Argento, or Led Zeppelin bootlegs, or literary criticism, or sailboats, or arguments between devotees of manga and anime, or really anything else people care about deeply. No passion can be understood from the outside.

When an unexpected glimpse of a Michigan football helmet no longer moves me, in ways that might seem strange or irrational, I will know that an important part of me has died—that part of me that remains most closely connected to the boy I once was. Genuine fandom is, among other things, a way of never growing up. That can obviously be a bad thing. Still it has been observed that, unless you are converted and become as little children, you will by no means enter the kingdom of heaven.

THE FACTORY
OF SADNESS

At age three, my son became intensely interested in garbage trucks. When I was a child, a similar obsession would have been limited to running out to the curb to shake the truck driver's hand and perhaps taking an occasional trip to the local dump.

But because we live in the age of the Internet, we were together able to pursue his passion in a much more comprehensive way. For instance, the two of us discovered that there is a rich subculture of people—usually middle-aged men—who dedicate themselves to filming garbage trucks in action and then uploading their work to YouTube. The number of such videos is in the thousands. A single auteur—the cinematic visionary behind Thrash & Trash Productions—has produced dozens, including a compilation that by itself features 135 different types of garbage trucks in action. (This work could perhaps be considered the *Citizen Kane* of the genre.) Because of such efforts, both my son and I can now readily distinguish a Curotto Screaming Eagle from a Peterbilt 320 Heil DuraPack and a Mack MRU 450X from a Volvo WX64.

The British term "anorak" describes this general phenomenon. In the 1980s, the term was first applied to trainspotters—people who would stand for hours on station platforms and along railroad tracks, to record in the most obsessive detail every feature of passing trains. An anorak is a kind of parka, often worn by trainspotters in frigid conditions. From there, "anorak" came to mean anyone who engaged in the obsessive pursuit of any marginal niche interest: analogous terms in other cultures include the Spanish *friki* and the Japanese *otaku*. The American slang terms "geek" and "nerd" can be used similarly but typically have broader, less precise connotations.

It has been speculated that anoraks display a type of high-functioning autism, manifested as an obsessive focus on their particular interest, with this focus often impeding the sort of social responses and interactions considered normal or appropriate by neurologically typical people. The Internet has made it much easier for anoraks to pursue their passions. And it also has made it much easier for otherwise neurologically typical people to become anoraks, at least for short periods.

In any event, during Michigan football games, many otherwise normal board denizens become anoraks of a conspiratorial nature. (I know because I'm one of them.) It generally takes just a few minutes—often only a play or two—for a group of highly educated, ordinarily reasonable, and otherwise unexceptionable people to decompensate into a bunch of raving lunatics. Shared suffering quickly morphs into collective madness, as we—usually unintentionally—egg each other on toward ever more elaborate manifestations of conspiratorial thinking, histrionic complaining, and other florid displays of our communal masochism.

If the game is close—that is, if victory isn't already almost assured—or, God forbid, Michigan is actually losing, then the board will become a veritable bedlam of agonized cries about terrible coaching decisions, poor officiating, inept play, and the existence of a universal conspiracy to ensure that Michigan will ultimately lose. This conspiracy can include the crooked or blind refs, the league office (which mysteriously wants one of the league's best-known and profitable programs to fail), and the egregiously dirty players on the other team (who are obviously a bunch of thugs who would never be recruited by our coaches). Our coaches, by the way, totally suck, because they never ever learn from their mistakes, though we point them out constantly. They are almost as bad as the network television commentators, who everybody knows have always hated us, or the opposing fans, who are classless idiots who couldn't get into Michigan—not that "our" students are any better, given that they can't be bothered to show up on time or create any home field advantage by actually making noise. Ultimately the entire board turns on itself, with accusations flying among ridiculously optimistic "sunshine blowers" or absurdly pessimistic "excellence demanders." For as long as this mental state lasts (i.e., until Michigan has an unquestionably safe lead), we hate everything and everybody, especially ourselves, as we wallow in the realization that, once again, we are choosing to waste our lives in this pathetic way.

In other words, during a game, the board is a prime example of how the Internet makes it easy for obsessives to feed off each other so that their obsession becomes, individually and collectively, increasingly intense and unhinged. Indeed, some posters who seem quite normal under ordinary circumstances can appear, under the extraordinary stress of watching a college football game, genuinely mentally ill.

Of course, I assume the latter category doesn't actually include myself, which is an easy assumption to make, since on the Internet there is always someone crazier. This is because there is always someone who is more knowledgeable, more obsessive, and more addicted than you are. I've mentioned my friend Rich, who is one of the board's moderators. He not only knows the exact starting times of old Michigan games; he knows whether Michigan wore white or maize pants as part of its road football uniform in 1979, how many times "we" have lost to Iowa over the past fifty seasons, and more. He doesn't have to google any this either: he just knows it. While I can recite the final score of every Michigan–Ohio State football game from the 1970s off the top of my head or tell you what happened to the first pass Tom Brady threw at Michigan (it was picked off and returned for a touchdown by a UCLA defensive back), Rich always makes me feel like a dilettante in regard to all things Michigan. He makes me feel, as it were, perfectly normal, even though both of us are obviously at least a little insane.

Another thing I have learned over the course of a quarter century on the board is that the board itself is, when it comes to the almost endless number of ways an obsession with Michigan football can manifest itself on the Internet, very much the tip of an iceberg. For instance, the board is only tangentially involved with the entire subculture that follows college football recruiting—the pursuit of the high school stars who will become part of next year's team (or, increasingly, of teams two and three years down the road, as the recruiting system comes to focus on players at ever-earlier stages of their careers). Dozens of sites are dedicated to following recruiting battles between schools. Uncounted numbers of middle-aged men obsess over the inevitably fickle preferences of seventeen-year-old high school football players. On numerous pay sites, self-certified recruiting gurus parcel out nuggets of information, or purported information, about whether a "five-star" linebacker from Valdosta, Georgia, who was "leaning" toward Alabama earlier in the week, is now "leaning" toward coming to Ann Arbor, after the "in-home" visit from Michigan's coaches. (For only $9.99 per month, you can get access to these nuggets several minutes before they become available for free across the rest of the Internet.)

Indeed, some people seem far more interested in recruiting battles than in the outcomes of actual college football games. This particularly weird subgenre of fans—but again, who am I to talk?—seems to root for Michigan to win on the field primarily because that makes it more likely that the school will triumph in the battle for future talent. A similar reversal can be seen among certain NFL fans, who seem to be more obsessed with the annual player draft than with the subsequent action on the field. Pecuniary and ego-driven considerations create a more readily understandable form of this psychological reversal, when fantasy football team owners become far more interested in their fantasy teams than in any real—or, I suppose, "real"—NFL team.

It's now possible to be obsessed with every aspect of sports—with strategic decisions, with personnel management, with statistical analysis, with interpersonal drama, with economic considerations, and so on and so forth—to an extent that far exceeds what was possible before the Internet transformed the sports world into a bar that never closes, where the most passionate and unhinged fans argue about every conceivable subject. As a teenager in the 1970s, I remember waiting until well into the summer to buy the three or four available preseason college football magazines. These constituted my first information about the coming season. I particularly remember the excitement and anticipation that surrounded the arrival of *Sports Illustrated*'s preview issue, which my brothers and I would scour to learn Michigan's preseason ranking, as well as what sages thought of our players, many of whose names we would be recalling for the first time in months.

Now there is literally hundreds of times more information about Michigan football available on the phone in my pocket than I could have found anywhere in the entire world, even if I had had unlimited time and money, back when my passion for the team first bloomed during my official adolescence. For example, MGOBLOG, a site founded and maintained by Brian Cook, a single dedicated Michigan fan, analyzes the performance of every player on every play of every Michigan game during the season with a level of granularity and sophistication inconceivable a generation ago. And there are countless similar sites, feeding the obsessions of the deeply engaged fans of teams in every major sport.

There is of course a dark side to this technological revolution. The Internet not only reveals both the sheer variety and extraordinary depth of human obsession; it also intensifies those obsessions by bringing the obsessed together into an omnipresent community, which can therefore become surprisingly difficult to avoid. This can easily turn what were once harmless hobbies into far from harmless addictive relationships.

The historian David Courtwright has coined the term "limbic capitalism" to describe the many ways in which contemporary Big Tech uses advanced communication technologies to create and then supply ever more elaborate forms of addiction. Courtwright argues that Internet-linked mobile devices in particular now operate like gambling machines or drug dispensers: "You're constantly getting dinged, you're constantly getting messages, you're concerned about likes, you're wondering about the latest post, you have this fear of missing out." In particular he points to the structural effects of smartphones, which both supply access to the substance of various addictions and actively condition people to acquire what can easily become self-destructive habits—including most notably an addiction to these devices themselves. "Smartphone technologies," he asserts, "arguably accomplish this better than any device or product in human history."

Fifty years ago, the main character in Frederick Exley's novelistic memoir *A Fan's Notes*—a drinker with a writing problem, hopelessly devoted to the New York Giants football team—concluded that alcoholism is sadness. After a quarter century on the board, I have concluded that a life lived on the Internet is not too different from what Exley depicts as "that long malaise, my life."

Consider a post from an Ohio State message board, the morning after OSU had lost to Clemson in the semifinals of the college football playoffs at the end of the 2016 season. At that moment, Ohio State's coach, Urban Meyer, had won sixty-one of his sixty-seven games in his five years at the school. This had given OSU the best record of any team in the sport over that same span; he had also won the national championship two years earlier. Taking into account his earlier similarly spectacular stints at Florida, Utah, and Bowling Green, Meyer was at that point quite arguably the most successful coach in college football history; at a minimum, he was on a very short list for that distinction.

Here is what one deeply engaged Buckeye fan had to say, after having had a chance to sleep on the Clemson loss: "Urban Meyer has become Michigan's Rich Rod[riguez], with better players and a decent defense." (Rodriguez's tenure at Michigan had been a complete disaster; he lost 33 percent more games in his first season alone than Meyer had lost in five full seasons at Ohio State.) The replies to the post mostly concurred with this sober assessment. These words were posted more in sadness than in anger, because sadness is the characteristic emotion of all deeply engaged fans lost in cyberspace, just as surely as that emotion dominates the lives those who battle the bottle, or the needle, or whatever other demon has got them in its sway.

For the truth is that, for passionate fans, no amount of previous success can keep our faith from collapsing at any moment. That is why we live in constant dread of the fate we know awaits us. We live on the Internet, and while the Internet is many things, for people like us it is above all a factory of sadness.

LOSE YOURSELF

A deeply engaged fan's imaginative life is in no small part formed by the memory of the worst losses—of those moments when fandom truly seems to be nothing but folly. So it is that, for we Michigan football fans who came of age in the early 1970s, the scars of the four Ohio State games played between 1972 and 1975 run especially deep. These were my earliest teenage years, and the first Ohio State games I actually saw on TV or—in the case of the infamous 10–10 tie in 1973—in person. Each of these games ended up being a case study in the cruelest sort of experience that sporting events can visit on impressionable young minds.

1972: An undefeated Michigan team loses when Harry Banks crosses the goal line not once but twice for what would have been the winning touchdown. Yet the referee will not raise his hands either time! I can still hear the feverish outrage in Bob Ufer's voice, as we watched the telecast with the sound turned down and the radio turned up, as he describes this travesty in gruesome detail and points out that it's exactly like another act of officiating robbery that took place in Columbus twenty years earlier.

1973: An undefeated Michigan team clearly outplays the top-ranked Buckeyes, yet Mike Lantry misses two field goals in the closing minutes, thereby snatching a tie from the jaws of victory. The next day, the Big Ten athletic directors vote to send Ohio State, not Michigan, to the Rose Bowl. I still remember with Rain Man–like clarity the precise moment when I heard this news during the NFL game I was watching.

1974: An undefeated Michigan team loses in Columbus again when Lantry attempts a short field goal as time expires. The kick is good, but inexplicably the officials claim it isn't. In an uncomprehending rage at the injustice of the world, I sweep a half-completed thousand-piece jigsaw puzzle off the dining room table.

1975: An undefeated Michigan team loses to the top-ranked Buckeyes again after leading late into the fourth quarter. All-American linebacker Calvin O'Neal drops what would have been a game-clinching interception.

This was my introduction to genuine fandom: an entire season of nothing but victory, building up to one climactic all-deciding game (At the time, Big Ten teams were only allowed to play in the Rose Bowl, so if "we" lost the Ohio State game, the season was over at that moment, with at least four months of Michigan winter directly ahead.) The 1972 through 1974 Michigan teams lost a total of two of the thirty-three games they played, and still never got to play in a bowl game. Forty-five years later, I can recite these facts as readily as a nun can say the rosary.

The tenderness of youth ensured that those Ohio State games will remain the deepest scars of my fandom, but memory allows other limbless monsters of pain to unfold themselves any time I fall into the sort of masochistic reverie that any deeply engaged fan will recognize. For example, take the 2015 Michigan—Michigan State game. Michigan had the ball and the lead with ten seconds left, in Michigan State territory. Ten seconds! I was yelling at the TV—just snap the ball and run around for a bit! I mean how hard can that be? But no: coach Jim Harbaugh decides to play it "safe" by punting. Because Michigan State players are a bunch of thugs who could never get into Michigan, one of them—totally illegally, I will add—slaps Michigan's center in the head as he's snapping the ball, leading to a bad snap that bounces on the ground in front of our punter, who is from Australia and doesn't really understand the rules of American football apparently. (He had been brought onto the team to be a new-fangled Australian Rules Football–type punter, who scurries toward the sideline and delivers a rugby-style kick. This is supposed to be more effective than the traditional punting style, and our innovative coach had decided to innovate in this ultimately fatal way.)

Anyway, all the punter has to do is fall on the ball. If he does, then the worst-case scenario, assuming time doesn't actually expire before the end of this play, is that MSU gets the ball at midfield with time for a Hail Mary pass to the end zone (probability of success: approximately 2 percent). But no: the punter—I'm actually blocking his name out at the moment—O'Neill? Or am I confusing him with the O'Neal from the 1975 OSU game?—suddenly starts acting like he's a fan who won some sort of contest to participate in one play in a major college football game. In a spastic panic, he attempts to kick the ball, even as he's being overwhelmed by waves of Spartans in a sort of reverse Thermopylae.

Of course the kick is blocked, and, following the inexorable logic of certain nightmares, it bounces at just the right angle into the arms of the one MSU player who is in position to run unimpeded toward the Michigan end zone. I keep thinking that maybe he'll miraculously fall down, or an asteroid or an ICBM will strike the stadium in the next five seconds, but none of these things happen. Afterward, Michigan State's coach, the intolerable Mark Dantonio—a person whose visage at all times and in every circumstance is that of a man undergoing a colonoscopy—*actually runs to the base of the Michigan student section and starts taunting the crowd*. In yet another gross injustice from that miserable afternoon, he is not immediately lynched.

Or consider the 1994 Colorado game. By that time I had been on the Colorado faculty for several years, but this didn't make the slightest difference to my college football loyalties, which could not be affected by something as trivial as my professional identity. This time, there are six seconds left. For the last two minutes of the game— this is in football time, in astronomical time this interval took many agonizing minutes to play—I have been calculating exactly how long Colorado will have to score a touchdown if they get the ball back. Six seconds. Surely their quarterback, Kordell Stewart, cannot throw the ball the 70 yards that will be required to get the ball to the end zone on the game's last play? He can. The ball hangs in the air for what seems like approximately half an hour, and, during this time, I suddenly have a strangely serene, almost Zen-like sense that it's going to be caught by a Colorado receiver. Michael Westbrook, a Detroit native (traitor), does catch it, with future Pro Football Hall of Fame cornerback Ty Law hanging desperately onto his shoulders.

I'm sitting in front of the TV in Boulder, and, within three seconds of the catch, I have turned it off. I then do something that would be impossible to do now, twenty-six years later: I go into a complete information blackout. For days, I do not look at a television or a newspaper. (The Internet, let alone social media, doesn't really exist yet.) Through heroic self-discipline, I manage to go more than a year before ever seeing a replay of this event, even though the play had surely by then been rebroadcast hundreds of times on local and national media.

Indeed, so thoroughly do I manage to avoid any reliving of this event that it becomes in some way fundamentally unreal to me—so much so that, the next summer, I have an uncanny experience on the Boulder campus. I'm walking to the main library, and I see a student wearing a T-shirt featuring an image of Kordell Stewart and the words "Trailing 26–21, 6 seconds to go, 70 yards from the end zone, no problem." For a couple of seconds I have an indescribably eerie sensation that this T-shirt is somehow describing a nightmare I once had. Only then do I remember the truth I have so successfully repressed.

Today, this story could never happen. Back then, I had the option of suffering alone and pretending to myself that the catastrophe was something I could choose to ignore. Today, deeply engaged fans cannot really choose to be alone: the Internet is always there, irresistibly beckoning, making a psychological offer we can't refuse. Even—indeed especially—the most excruciating losses must immediately be relived, relitigated, and essentially experienced over and over again, in some perverse version of the Hindu or Nietzschean cycle of eternal return. (Perhaps for my sins I will be reincarnated as a Cleveland Browns fan.)

Does this communal reexperience of our initial grief exacerbate it, or cleanse us of it through a kind of cathartic purging? Probably both: in any case, it is now unavoidable, unless we choose to stop caring at all—which remains about as realistic an option for us as it does for addicts of any other persuasion.

And yet . . . I am back in Michigan, on an almost supernaturally perfect fall weekend. Jim Harbaugh, has, against all odds, left behind his extremely successful tenure as an NFL head coach to return to his alma mater in its hour of greatest need and, after the previous seven seasons of increasingly ludicrous disasters, the team is once again looking like it did during the previous forty years, when it failed to win at least two-thirds of its games only twice.

It's Friday night, and before heading to Ann Arbor, I accompany my brother into the wilderness of rural Michigan (specifically the village of Schoolcraft, population 1,525), to watch the Schoolcraft Eagles battle the Gobles Tigers. The Eagles are something of a football powerhouse among schools of their size, having won the state championship a few years earlier.

We sit close to Benny Clark Jr., at one time the leading rusher in Michigan high school football history, to whom my brother is connected by the vagaries of marital fortune and misfortune (His ex-wife's sister is Benny's former wife.) Twenty years earlier, Benny's team defeated the Eagles in the state championship game. Now his son Boom Boom is Schoolcraft's star running back.

Benny's immediate family makes up approximately half of Schoolcraft's African American population, and Boom Boom, who is about 5 foot 9 and cannot weigh more than 145 pounds, is the fastest player on the field by an almost comical margin. Around half of his carries go for at least 20 yards until the score has grown so lopsided that, per the sensible rules employed in Michigan high school football in such situations, the game clock runs continuously.

Benny is surrounded by a posse of middle-aged former warriors of the Friday night lights, and the unambiguous enjoyment they all take in Boom Boom's exploits is infectious. We cheer each of his four long touchdown runs with childlike enthusiasm, and I think of James Wright's "Autumn Begins in Martins Ferry, Ohio":

> *In the Shreve High football stadium,*
> *I think of Polacks nursing long beers in Tiltonsville,*

And gray faces of Negroes in the blast furnace at Benwood,
And the ruptured night watchman of Wheeling Steel,
Dreaming of heroes.

At halftime, an ensemble combining the Schoolcraft high school band with those of various area middle schools performs a version of Fleetwood Mac's "Tusk." (The original version featured the University of Southern California marching band.) The noise is indescribable. After the game, we walk to our car through the crisp autumn night air, and at least for one evening my feelings about small-town Americana are more John Mellencamp than Bruce Springsteen.

The next morning I drive to Ann Arbor. The weather again is ideal: while meteorological conditions in Michigan range from mediocre to miserable on roughly three hundred days per year, residents are recompensed with the occasional amazing fall day, with temperatures in the low 60s (optimal for watching football outside), crystalline blue skies, and the beauty of the autumn leaves, which bring to mind Keats and Yeats at their most elegiac.

I'm sitting again with Rich, and beforehand we stop at fellow board fixture GoBrew Bob's sumptuous tailgate. Bob is a beer maven of the first order, and his tailgate always provides an opportunity to sample some outrageously good bit of Belgian or American microbrew exotica. The food and the drink are enhanced by the presence of several other board members; these rare meetings outside of cyberspace are always a bit disorienting at first, but soon we overwhelm each other with enthusiasm for the dawn of the Harbaugh era, along with slyly competitive discussions about Michigan teams past and present. It's always a bit annoying when a fellow fanatic conveys some piece of information about the present team—an injury or a benching or a transfer—that I didn't already know.

Later, the game itself turns out to be almost a Platonic ideal of an autumn afternoon at Michigan Stadium. The weather remains perfect; the opponent, Northwestern, is ranked thirteenth in the country, more than respectable, and the action itself turns out to be one of those rare occasions when even the board—which we cannot access, as Internet connectivity in the Stadium is terrible—will struggle to find much to complain about.

The first fifteen seconds of the game capture the essence of the experience. Just before the kickoff, the Stadium's loudspeakers blast out the hypnotic guitar riff from the beginning of Eminem's "Lose Yourself," and a low guttural roar starts to build out of the student section. I normally despise the practice of bombarding the crowd with music during sporting events, but in this instance it somehow fits the moment perfectly, and we are all swept up by the sense of collective belonging that has been exploited so successfully by everyone from fascists to football coaches.

The kickoff sails down to Jehu Chesson at the 4-yard line: he cuts across the field, finds a wall of blockers, and sails down the sideline all the way to the end zone. 110,452 voices (minus a smattering of Northwestern fans) merge into a wave of bleacher-quivering noise, and for the next three hours and twenty minutes we are in that rarest state for any deeply engaged fan: total, unsullied joy, as Michigan goes on to a crushing 38–0 win.

A mere seven days later the same fans will experience one of the worst losses in the team's history, in the Michigan State game I described above. But that moment, along with countless other traumas and travails of fandom, remains safely in the unknown and temporarily impotent future.

So happiness is possible, even for us, the deeply engaged—which is to say for the neurotic seekers of a kind of perfection that sports, like life itself, so rarely provide.

ME AND MRS. JONES

Once upon a time, near the beginning of my academic career, I took part in hiring a more senior professor away from an Ivy League school to the University of Colorado. Dale was and is an accomplished corporations law scholar—a field I know almost nothing about. We did have an area of shared expertise, however: Michigan football.

Both of us have three degrees from the University of Michigan, and we both went to every home football game during our respective tenures in Ann Arbor. In addition, Dale had been in a quasi-secret society, whose roll included several prominent members of the football team. This detail made his prestige, in my eyes, very great. This was one reason I had pushed so hard to hire him. And yes, I realize this is exactly the sort of factor that gives men in general unfair advantages over women in many evaluative contexts.

During the recruiting process, we had several conversations about the golden age of Michigan football, a.k.a. our respective youths. Thus it didn't surprise me that, a few weeks after he had settled into his new office next door to mine, he asked me about our chances of winning the season opener that coming Saturday. I said that Notre Dame was always a tough opponent, especially in South Bend, but I was still optimistic. He replied, "No, I meant Colorado."

My shock was profound. "Dale," I wanted to say, "you've been here for three weeks. What do you mean 'we'?" Because I was still untenured I chose to maintain a discreet silence regarding this shameless philandering. In all matters of fandom, I was and remain stubbornly monogamous. I take no undue pride in this: my inability to transfer my affections to other teams is no more praiseworthy than the fact that I get no thrill from gambling, and therefore am never tempted to indulge in that particular vice. I still, however, feel quite censorious toward fans who do cheat on their teams.

Front running—rooting for a team because it is successful—is the opposite of genuine fandom, as every deeply engaged fan recognizes almost instinctually. Thus Michigan State fans mock what they call "Wal-Mart Wolverines"—Michigan fans whose socioeconomic status is well below that of the typical Michigan graduate and who are therefore assumed to have come by their Michigan fandom dishonestly rather than organically. This distinction is one of the more mysterious aspects of the whole business. The categorical imperative that guides the ethics of fandom seems to be that rooting for a successful team is legitimate only to the extent that the fan in question didn't consciously choose to root for the team because of its success. Thus the earlier in life an allegiance is acquired, the better.

Although I very much enjoy watching high-level European soccer, I confess to a certain skepticism of people who, in middle age, somehow develop what they present as a deep engagement with the Barcelona or Liverpool or Juventus football clubs or a genuine passion for Tottenham Hotspur or Paris Saint-Germain. Such late-in-life enthusiasms are a little too reminiscent of the posturing of sportswriter Bill Simmons, who a few years back announced he had decided to adopt a Premier League club to follow and solicited nominations from his readers as to who should become the object of his consciously acquired passion in this interesting new—to him—sports league. *It doesn't work like that*, I thought.

Nothing demonstrates the inadequacy of a consumption model of fandom better than the centrality of this concept of fan loyalty. Consider how strange it would be to criticize someone for ceasing to patronize a restaurant because a better, cheaper restaurant had opened across the street, or for no longer going to, say, Steven Spielberg films, because they had become stale and repetitive. In the world of ordinary consumer behavior, the idea that it's positively praise-worthy to give one's allegiance to a product that used to be good but is now bad is incomprehensible on its face.

Yet in the world of fandom, analogous reasoning is considered to be not only defensible, but self-evidently valid. Real fans don't abandon their team just because it's bad: indeed, the worse the team has become, the more its current state provides an acid test. It's a complex process, but you have to earn your fandom honestly: true fandom is, by definition, for better and for worse. The legitimacy of the fan's affection is determined, above all, by an ongoing demonstra-tion of loyalty when the team struggles to win.

From a utilitarian perspective, it makes sense to root for a team precisely because it wins, and to cease doing so when it doesn't. The founder of utilitarianism, the English philosopher Jeremy Bentham, would, if he were around today, probably advocate switching alle-giances every time the lead changed hands in the course of a game, if not from play to play (Nietzsche on utilitarian philosophers: "Man does not seek pleasure, only the Englishman does"). But of course such strategic behavior makes no sense from the perspective of fan-dom, because deeply engaged fans aren't seeking the pleasures of consumption but rather the cleansing power of catharsis, which is intimately connected to pain.

During an especially close NFL playoff game in January 2020, a board poster remarked how watching it was positively enjoyable, re-gardless of the result. "It's so much more fun to watch when you don't really care very much who wins," he noted. Indeed it is. The shallow engagement of the casual fan is much more pleasurable to experience than the emotional stress of deep engagement. The latter is, for the most part, a source of anxiety, pain, and frustration, which we can only hope will be alleviated at some point by a sense of relief, as the drug once more courses through our veins.

For me, the difference between deep and shallow engagement is captured perfectly by the contrast between my experience of football games involving, on the one hand, Michigan, and, on the other, the NFL's Denver Broncos. I am, in the ordinary sense of the word, a fan of the Broncos: I watch all their games, I unambivalently want them to win those games, and I even listen, in my car, to a good amount of sports radio commentary regarding the team. Sports radio in the Denver area devotes approximately 97 percent of its time to the Broncos. When I first came to Colorado in 1990, I soon realized that a typical newspaper headline was "Elway Feels Tightness in Hamstring." I'm also a Broncos fan because my wife is: for many decades her family has gathered on Sunday afternoons to watch the team's games and share a communal meal, and we've continued to participate in this ritual.

But ultimately, what being a Broncos fan—I feel a strong urge to put scare quotes around the word "fan" in this context—has taught me is what it is to be what is now often referred to as a "normie." Compared to the existential terror of watching a Michigan football game, a Broncos game is vastly more enjoyable. I *want* the Broncos to win, but I don't *need* them to win. Ten minutes after Denver lost the Super Bowl to Seattle in 2014, I was no longer thinking about the game. The next day I probably couldn't have told you the final score; meanwhile, forty-seven years later, I'm still thinking about the 1974 Ohio State game and can describe not just the final score but how each of those twenty-two points came about.

The 2016 Michigan–Ohio State game, and Denver's game the next day with Kansas City, provide an almost satanically perfect illustration of the contrast between catharsis and consumption: both were critical games to the teams' respective seasons, both games went into overtime, and both were lost by "my" team by the identical score. The former loss was one of the most excruciating experiences of my life; the latter produced a brief mildly unpleasant sensation, like being forced to listen to one of Billy Joel's more aggravating songs. My wife, who sincerely considers herself a real Broncos fan, and who unlike me was once a highly successful competitive athlete, was literally asleep on the couch at the end of the Denver game. She finds my antics during Michigan games to be the height of childishness, which they no doubt are. "You're such a sore loser because you never learned to lose in real games," she tells me, which sounds annoyingly plausible.

My "positionality," as the anthropologists say, relative to the Broncos allows me to experience my fandom from a classic inside/outside perspective: in the end, like Margaret Mead in Samoa or Clifford Geertz in Bali, I'm more of a participant-observer than a real fan. In this context, I'm performing fandom more than actually living it. A casual ethnographer of the genuine passion others have for the Broncos, I'm grateful to the team and its fans for entertaining me. Still, when I listen to the agonized voices of real fans on talk radio the day after a bad loss—and of course for real fans they're all bad losses—I recognize that my fandom for the Broncos is more voyeuristic than genuine.

My youngest brother—a professional historian whose allegiance to Michigan football is similar to mine in its depth—has become increasingly cynical about the absurdity of fandom in general. (Indeed, he coined the phrase "fandom is folly" and encouraged me to pursue the subject.) In the fall of 2019, after a particularly frustrating Michigan game—one of those wins over a bad team that promises various baroque disasters are soon in store against better opposition—he called me with an idea: Why not just choose a "side team" to root for over the course of the season?

This side team could not, of course, be someone in Michigan's immediate orbit: it had to be somebody like Alabama or LSU: superbly talented teams that were also fun to watch play and who were extremely unlikely to play Michigan in any particular season. Rooting for such a team, he pointed out, would be fun. It would make the college football season as a whole much more enjoyable. It almost certainly wouldn't interfere with our primary fandom. Of course, in what might be interpreted by the superstitious as retribution for my brother's flagrant advocacy of infidelity, and my willingness to consider it, Michigan ended up playing—and getting trounced by—Alabama in a bowl game at the end of the 2019 season.

Still, at the time, all of this sounded eminently sensible, and more than a little tempting. But in the end, it's not something a deeply engaged fan can really do. I mean, you can always have an affair, but if your side team is just another casual jump-off, then the satisfactions of shallow engagement, such as they are, will do nothing to ameliorate the pain and frustration of your primary relationship. And if you should somehow start to get deeply engaged with the new object of your affection, you are setting yourself up for the sorts of emotional disasters chronicled in so many classic novels about adultery and its discontents.

Note that technology has made possible an arguably even shabbier form of infidelity: the DVR affair. This is consummated by short-circuiting both the agony and ecstasy of deep engagement, by recording the Big Game and then watching it only if your team wins. This is a particularly pathetic genre of cheating: a cowardly dodging of the most painful moments of fandom, but at the cost of maintaining an authentic and committed relationship. I confess that I have done this, but only a time or two.

Discussions with my brother led me to ponder a key question about the nature of deeply engaged fandom: Is it really possible to change your identity in this regard? Over the course of my life I have met liberals who used to be conservatives and Catholics who used to be Communists, and even women who used to be considered men. But I have never met a Michigan fan who used to be an Ohio State fan or vice versa. Indeed, the very idea seems in some fundamental way absurd.

Sociologists have argued that perhaps the most essential difference between traditional and modern societies is that, in the latter, it's possible to take on a new identity. For example, in *The Passing of Traditional Society*, Daniel Lerner's study of the mid-twentieth century Middle East, Lerner noted that many of the illiterate villagers he interviewed could only respond with laughter when asked what they would do if they were to change places with their rulers, and they would not even consider the question of under what circumstances they would leave their native village. Both these possibilities seemed to them almost literally unthinkable.

In our contemporary world, by contrast, nothing seems more natural than the possibility of radical personal change. But only to a point: I can imagine becoming an Englishman, or a Muslim, or (barely) a Trump voter, but I cannot, for example, imagine changing my gender identity. That identity seems to me in some way identical with my sense of self in a way that, unlike other, more contingent aspects of that self, is not separable from it. My identity as a Michigan fan really does feel as intrinsic to me as my sense of my gender, un-like my political or national affiliation. In other words, a conversion experience on that front is, to me, literally unimaginable. I cannot think of my fandom as mutable; as a consequence, I must reject any notion that a genuine Michigan fan could ever be anything else.

In the end, I agree with Nick Hornby, who argues that, when it comes to deeply engaged fandom, loyalty is "not a moral choice like bravery or kindness" but rather "something you were stuck with." Marriages, he notes, are not nearly as rigid: "You won't catch any Arsenal fans slipping off to Tottenham for a bit of extra-marital slap and tickle, and although divorce is a possibility (you can just stop go-ing if things get too bad), getting hitched again is out of the question."

VENTURA HIGHWAY

I'm just old enough to remember the 1970s American sports world, especially in its televised form. My parents had emigrated from Mexico a few months before I was born at the tail end of the baby boom, and they had no real knowledge of or interest in that world. I believe they could have told me who Babe Ruth was, but that would have been about it. So, as the oldest child in a family of five boys and one girl, it fell to me to discover this particular world on my own.

My very first memory of Michigan football is from the morning of November 23, 1969, seeing pictures of roses bordering the front page of the *Ann Arbor News* and asking my parents what that meant. My father, who worked at the university, explained that the school's football team was going to something called the Rose Bowl. The day before, Michigan had beat a heavily favored Ohio State team in what is still generally regarded as the greatest upset victory in the school's 140-year history in the sport. This epochal event took place all of five miles from me but I didn't even know that my father's employer had a football team until that morning.

I had just turned ten, and my ignorance of American sports was so complete that, the month before, I first learned about one of the greatest upsets in baseball history when Mrs. Wade, my fifth-grade teacher, a New Yorker, regaled the class with a tale of how her beloved New York Mets had just defeated the Baltimore Orioles in the World Series. Three months later Kansas City defeated Minnesota in the Super Bowl; I was also completely unaware of this event at the time.

My disconnection from the world of sports was so complete that I don't think I even knew what the Super Bowl—the highest of holy days in the American sports calendar—even was.

The next spring my father took the three oldest boys to a baseball game at Tiger Stadium in Detroit. This was of course a very memorable experience: like countless other kids I have a vivid memory of walking through the tunnel and seeing the immense space of a major league baseball field for the first time. I also remember feeling vaguely sorry for the old man wearing wire-rim glasses playing for the Washington Senators. He reminded me of my grandfather. This turned out to be Frank Howard: he was then thirty-three years old and would lead the league in home runs that season, one of which he hit that afternoon.

In October I watched the first game of the World Series and still have a clear memory, fifty years later, of Baltimore's third baseman Brooks Robinson robbing Cincinnati's Lee May of a double with a fantastic defensive effort. At around the same time I started watching Detroit Lions football games—I think the first game I ever saw featured the New Orleans Saints kicker Tom Dempsey making a record 63-yard field goal to win the game on its last play. This record would last for more than forty years and would prove a fitting introduction to the almost unparalleled futility of rooting for the Lions. In an uncanny demonstration of the circle of sports life, many decades later my brother's young son became an equally fanatic Lions fan and experienced exactly the same exquisite agony when the Lions lost yet another contest on the last play of the game—and by exactly the same score—when Baltimore kicker Justin Tucker broke the same record by kicking a 66-yard field goal, which bounced off the crossbar before going through the uprights. The Lions would have won if the kick had traveled literally an inch less than it did.

I found myself being drawn into the world of sports from several directions. During a family summer road trip out west, I bought a paperback of *Ball Four*, Jim Bouton's memoir of a season as a marginal major league relief pitcher. This was probably a very inappropriate book for an eleven-year-old to read: Bouton made no secret of the seamier side of the life in the major leagues, and my horizons about all sorts of adult matters were abruptly expanded.

In September, our father took the older boys to our first Michigan football game—a 55–0 win over Virginia—and suddenly I was hooked, apparently for life. I suspect he took us to these games in an effort to acculturate his children to the country of their birth; neither he nor my mother would develop any genuine interest in American sports until much later.

In the remarkably short time that these sorts of conversions can take place in childhood, I was transformed in less than a year from someone who knew literally nothing about the subject into the most fanatical little sports fan in the neighborhood. Suddenly someone who hadn't known who Ty Cobb was could tell you both his lifetime batting average and how many batting titles he had won, as well as his teammate Sam Crawford's major record for most career triples. These were more impressive accomplishments in the pre-Google age.

But almost immediately, my chief passion among all the other passions in this brave new world became Michigan football. I listened to every game on the radio, and took every opportunity I could to secure a student ticket—these cost two dollars!—to games at the immense Michigan Stadium. Official capacity at that time was 101,001, and until the mid-1970s it was generally sold out only once a year.

The greatest treat of all, in that distant and primitive time, was the rare chance to see the winged helmet in all its glory appear on our new Sony Trinitron color TV, which had just replaced our fuzzy old black-and-white model. The Trinitron generated what was for the time a remarkably clear picture on its 12-inch screen. Our grandmother had given it to the family as a Christmas present in 1971—it cost the equivalent of approximately $2,000 in today's money.

Young people today would scarcely believe how difficult it was to actually view a sporting event then. It is now without exaggeration possible to watch more college football games in a single weekend than were broadcast during an entire calendar year. Additionally, there was a whole raft of complex rules about how often even the most popular teams could appear on television: for most of the decade, the quota was no more than three times in two years. This meant that, in a typical season, we would get to see Michigan football on TV exactly once.

There was, however, one delightful exception to this otherwise parsimonious system: New Year's Day, when the networks broadcast all four major bowl games in succession. And the most magical of moments came when Michigan would appear in the Rose Bowl—the Granddaddy of Them All, as NBC's announcers never ceased to remind us—in the Arroyo Seco in Pasadena, California.

It's difficult to convey now what watching the Rose Bowl was like back then. For one thing, imagine Michigan in winter in the time before we felt the effects of climate change. The brutal, unending winters of the 1970s consisted of five straight months of bone-chilling cold, underneath a monotonous slate-gray sky that allowed the sun to appear for perhaps half an hour twice per month. The landscape itself was dominated by enormous drifts of slushy snow, that on a typical day were fed by an almost constant depressive staccato of tiny snowflakes, buffeted here and there by a wheedling, coat-piercing wind—the harbingers of the inevitable next big storm.

For another, keep in mind that the Rose Bowl was, as it were, It: You would not see another college football game until September. And I mean "not see" in a quite literal way, that is hard now to even imagine, as we loll in the decadent luxury of our present media-saturated age. There were not yet even any VCR tapes, let alone ESPN Classic replays, DVR recordings, or YouTube videos available to break our annual eight-month fast.

Most of all, the telecast of the Rose Bowl unveiled to us, as we huddled in practically Siberian if not Neolithic conditions, what appeared to be an almost mythical world, bathed in a warm golden light, where it was perpetually 77 degrees, and the girls from Beach Boys songs walked along a seashore that could easily be mistaken for paradise itself.

And here arises a question that literally never arose for me—or as far as I know for anyone else in my family—at the time: *Why didn't we go there?* I suspect that our collective failure to even consider the possibility reflected a kind of inherited Latin fatalism, combined perhaps with the sort of environmentally inculcated midwestern stoicism. Even more puzzling is the fact that I distinctly remember wondering at the time, when UCLA won a recruiting battle with Michigan for a running back from the Detroit area, how schools like Michigan and Ohio State, shivering in the increasingly depressed Rust Belt, ever won such battles against the sun-kissed glamor offered by the likes of USC and UCLA. Somehow this same puzzlement never extended to myself.

Yet it was that very failure to even contemplate the quintessentially American option of hitting the road and abandoning quasi-Siberia for the television's carefully curated vision of happiness, California-style, that gave the experience of watching the Rose Bowl on TV its peculiar melancholic power. There it was before us: the golden country, utterly unlike our own world, and yet connected to us by the temporary presence of those winged helmets that remained among the most recognizable symbols of our own miserable home, to which, like our football team—which always lost in the Rose Bowl when it made it that far—we remained so mysteriously loyal.

"It was long ago and far away, and it was so much better than it is today" is almost always at best a radical oversimplification, if not an outright lie. Still, there was something to be said for that otherwise absurd system that made watching a Michigan football game, and most especially the Rose Bowl, on TV one of life's most memorable moments.

I don't want to go back to that world—except to revisit the pain of an old wound, transformed by time into gauzy memories of our childhood, when we were so unhappy, between all the remembered parts.

THE POLITICS OF NOSTALGIA

In his book *The Historical Baseball Abstract*, Bill James has a recurring feature called "Old Ballplayers Never Die." It consists of quotes from old baseball players, drawn from many different decades, about how the game has gone downhill because of the decadence of the present generation. Here is Bill Joyce, a third baseman and manager in the 1890s, speaking in 1916:

> Baseball today is not what it should be. The players do not try to learn all the finer points of the game as in the days of old, but simply try to get by. They content themselves if they get a couple of hits every day or play an errorless game.
>
> When I was playing ball, there was not a move made on the field that did not cause every one of the opposing team to mention something about it. All were trying to figure out why it had been done and to see what the result would be. The same move could never be pulled again without every one on our bench knowing just what was going to happen.
>
> I feel sure that the same conditions do not prevail today. The boys go out to the plate, take a slam at the ball, pray that they'll get a hit, and let it go at that. They are not fighting as in the days of old. Who ever heard of a gang of ballplayers after losing going into the clubhouse singing at the top of their voices? That's what happens every day after the games of the present time.
>
> In my days, the players went into the clubhouse after losing a game with murder in their hearts. They would have thrown out any guy on his

neck if they had even suspected him of intentions of singing. In my days the man who was responsible for having lost the game was told in a man's way by a lot of men what a rotten ballplayer he really was. It makes me weep to think of the men of the old days who played the game and the boys of today.

It's positively a shame, and they are getting big money for it, too.

I thought of Joyce's ancient lament recently, when reading Kareem Abdul-Jabbar's thoughts on why scoring in the NBA is down, in comparison to the 1970s and 1980s, when he was one of the league's dominant players. For him, the explanation is that players today have poor fundamentals, because they no longer spend enough time in college learning their trade before jumping at the big money now available to them in the pros:

> When players of [my] era got to college, they had to earn playing time and to compete with upperclassmen. . . . Players also had to take the time to learn their coach's game plans for offense and defense before they were considered ready to play. . . . Add to this hierarchy the burden of going to class and taking the courses necessary to stay eligible and you had a system that made sure the players who were entering the NBA were knowledgeable about the game. In addition, the responsibilities they had to handle while at a university helped make them more mature and prone to have developed a work ethic during their college years. Making a transition to the professional ranks was much less challenging for those players.
>
> Players today are much less likely to have spent significant time in college. College basketball is not much more than a warm-up for the NBA draft for the most talented one [year]-and-done players. Too many of these players don't understand the subtle aspects of the game, and their undeniably outstanding athletic ability does them very little good when they struggle to learn the pro game in high-pressure circumstances.

All of this is obviously absurd on its face. For one thing, pointing to a decrease in scoring as evidence for a supposed decline in players' understanding of the game is exactly as plausible as pointing to an increase in scoring as evidence for the very same thing. Imagine: "Players today don't understand the finer points of defense, because they never had to learn them in college," etc.

For another, it's not hard to demonstrate that talented players today receive, and from the youngest age, far more extensive and sophisticated coaching than players did a generation ago. As someone who remembers the basketball of the 1970s fairly well, what I find especially bemusing about this particular trip down memory lane is how it presents that decade as a golden era of unselfish teammates and great fundamentals, as opposed to the chaotic cocaine-fueled bacchanal some of Kareem's less sentimental contemporaries might recall. A brief personal vignette from the era: one night at Cobo Hall in Detroit, the Pistons were playing the Knicks, and John Mengelt, a journeyman shooting guard for the Pistons, was off to a red-hot start. The Knicks' coaches then switched the nonpareil defender Walt "Clyde" Frazier onto Mengelt, who immediately cooled off considerably. As the two players were running down the court together in the second quarter, a gentleman attired in a full-length fur coat and a strikingly large-brimmed feathered hat stood up from his courtside seat and opened his coat with a flourish, revealing a pearl-handled revolver. "Clyde, don't be messin' with my man Mengelt," he advised Frazier. It was a simpler, more innocent time.

For deeply engaged fans in particular, sports are above all about memory. Thus nostalgia is the dominant emotion that marks our fandom. To be a fan is to be someone who spends much of his mental life trapped in the past. This has been driven home to me more than once when I've been asked what I'm thinking about, and, instead of being able to answer "climate change," or "our anniversary dinner," or even "whether I remembered to mail the mortgage payment," I've been reduced to either lying or confessing that the true answer has to do with a particularly glorious or painful moment in a college football game played several decades ago.

I have, obviously, nothing against nostalgia per se. In writing this book, what am I doing but, among other things, indulging my own nostalgic impulses at what some—including myself—might consider self-indulgent length? But we are now living in a culture that is positively saturated in nostalgia—and technology has made this possible in an unprecedented way. For the nostalgic life of the deeply engaged fan is just a subset of the countless ways in which it is becoming increasingly easy for everyone to become trapped by their past.

Consider YouTube music videos and the comments they elicit. (Almost five billion videos are watched on YouTube every single day.) To take an almost random example, listen to the two minutes and fifteen seconds of evanescent pop music perfection that is "Caroline No" (The Beach Boys, *Pet Sounds*, 1966), and then look at the comments from viewers. The third most popular out of many hundreds is this: "One of the greatest groups ever. How sad that we don't have that kind of inventive music anymore."

Almost literally every one of the innumerable great and not so great old and not so old songs on YouTube will feature many comments similar to this one. This particular genre of comments is so ubiquitous that it has generated its own subgenre of responses, critiquing the rampant nostalgia that dominates the site. The best one of these I've seen is a comment posted in response to the official video of Mazzy Star's ethereal ballad from the spring of 1994: "Fade into You." Amid dozens of paeans to how lead singer Hope Sandoval's hauntingly beautiful performance transports listeners back to that obviously superior musical era, Immaculate Spanish Kid remarks, "Welcome to the future . . . where everyone wants to live in the past." Precisely.

Popular culture has increasingly become in essence a kind of time machine that can hurl us deep into the irrecoverable past. Consider in this light the furious online arguments among fans of the *Star Wars* film franchise, about the quality and authenticity of each new entrant, compared to George Lucas's original canon. These arguments are so passionate in no small part because these fans are looking for what they can never find, which is the original unmediated thrill they experienced in childhood when they first encountered the *Star Wars* universe.

Indeed, it's difficult to overstate how much technology has intensified the experience of nostalgia. In November 1976, my brothers and I drove through the chilly midwestern night to sit on cold metal folding chairs, in a room in the Kalamazoo public library, as the local chapter of the Michigan alumni association presented a silent-film replay of the previous weekend's Ohio State game. We did this because we knew it would be our only chance to reexperience Michigan's epic victory in any medium other than our own memories.

Or so we thought. Today, I can watch the entire 1976 Michigan–Ohio State game—or any other Michigan–Ohio State game from the past half century—by simply taking my phone out of my pocket. And I occasionally do watch replays of forty-five-year-old Michigan games for the same reason I still occasionally listen to "Stairway to Heaven," even though I've heard at least parts of that song, conservatively, several thousand times. Yet every time I hear the sound of John Bonham's drum first join Jimmy Page's lead guitar line, I still get a shiver of the old original thrill, just as every time I see Rick Leach shed Tom Cousineau's arm tackle and dive across the goal line for the winning touchdown, a little bit of what I felt that gray day in the fall of 1977 comes back to me again. In both cases, these faint echoes of the original experience still retain some of their ephemeral magic, despite—or perhaps because of—the passage of the years. So we luxuriate in nostalgia, enjoying in the present even the pain of old wounds, transformed as they are by time and memory.

Still, while all this can seem harmless enough, it may seem less so when we consider the politics of the present moment. Nostalgia is by definition a reactionary state of mind. The nostalgia that increasingly saturates our experience of the present day compares the present to the past, and inevitably finds it wanting.

This is not to say that YouTube videos of 1970s football games, or classic rock radio stations, or the *Star Wars* franchise, or any other cultural remnants of the baby boom are themselves directly responsible for the reactionary backlash that is washing over our culture. But it is worth contemplating how recent technological advances have greatly inflamed the universal human desire to return to an idealized past, and how that desire itself is being manipulated, both by an economy selling us an endless stream of consumer goods and a political system peddling increasingly noxious ideologies.

For example, on the eve of the 2016 election, the historian John McNeill reminded us of how central the myth of a lost golden age has always been to fascist political movements:

> Italian and German fascism shared a strong commitment to the notion of national rebirth. Mussolini and Hitler encouraged their supporters to believe in lost (or stolen) greatness, in a glorious past. That could be long ago, as with the Roman Empire, which Mussolini liked to invoke, or only a couple of decades prior, as with the German Reich that was, according to Hitler, "stabbed in the back" in 1918. Trump makes this appeal to a golden age the centerpiece of his campaign, assuring audiences that only he can "make America great again."

Again, it would be an exaggeration to claim that a culture that becomes increasingly saturated in nostalgia necessarily becomes more vulnerable to the blandishments of fascist demagogues. But it is not hyperbole to point out that the intense romance American culture in general and baby boomer culture in particular have developed with the past has broader political implications.

If we are now living in a future in which everyone wants to live in the past, then we can be sure that past is being distorted by the power of nostalgia, which constantly reworks our own life histories and that of our country to make both more palatable to us than any strictly accurate historical accounting would allow. Exaggerating the virtues of the athletic, musical, and cinematic heroes of our youth is a relatively benign symptom of that tendency; nevertheless, the urge to do so is connected to other urges, many of which are not nearly so benign.

BEAUTIFUL LOSERS

One of the more memorable moments in American film is the opening scene of *Patton*. An enormous American flag fills the screen: the unseen troops of the Third Army are called to attention, and a bugle call sounds as the film's eponymous hero (played by George C. Scott) ascends onto a stage and into the center of the frame. He salutes the troops; in several successive still shots, the camera lingers on the decorations on Patton's uniform. The general then delivers a stirring monologue on the glories of war, beginning:

> I want you to remember that no bastard ever won a war by dying for his country. He won it by making the other poor, dumb bastard die for his country.
>
> Men, all this stuff you've heard about America not wanting to fight, wanting to stay out of the war, is a lot of horse dung. Americans, traditionally, love to fight. All real Americans love the sting of battle. When you were kids, you all admired the champion marble shooters, the fastest runners, big league ball players, the toughest boxers. *Americans love a winner and will not tolerate a loser.* Americans play to win all the time. I wouldn't give a hoot in hell for a man who lost and laughed. That's why Americans have never lost and will never lose a war, because the very thought of losing is hateful to Americans.
>
> Now, an army is a team. It lives, eats, sleeps, fights as a team. This individuality stuff is a bunch of crap. The bilious bastards who wrote that stuff

about individuality for the *Saturday Evening Post* don't know anything more about real battle than they do about fornicating.

It's a thrilling speech. It also sounds, today, at least a little like proto-fascist propaganda. (*Patton* was a reactionary rebuff to the national protest movement against the Vietnam War and was apparently Richard Nixon's favorite film. It also made a lot of money and won the Academy Award for Best Picture.)

Anyone who loves the spectacle of big-money team sports, especially football, should recognize that many aspects of that spectacle—the celebration of the individual merging into the larger whole in the pursuit of collective glory ("the team, the team, the team" has been the slogan of generals and coaches from time immemorial), the ecstatic identification of the spectators with that pursuit, the glorification of violent action for its own sake—have an uneasy resemblance to core features of classic fascist public ceremonies.

This is not to say that a big football game is genuinely analogous to a Nuremberg rally or that team sports in general, or football in particular, are actually fascistic rituals in even a loose sense. Still, in America, as in many other places around the world today, fascism is no longer just a subject for the history books. When we view *Patton* now, it is difficult not to notice that Scott's performance—his head often thrown back while his lip curls in an imperious sneer—gives him more than a passing resemblance to both Benito Mussolini and Donald Trump.

Yet while team sports are not inherently fascistic, certain aspects of the sports world lend themselves quite readily to ideological projects of the most dubious character. Football in particular seems to entangle itself with militarism, exceptionalism, the meritocratic American dream that creates so many temporarily embarrassed billionaires, and various other national myths, in an especially problematic way.

"Americans love a winner and will not tolerate a loser." Especially at the present moment, it is easy to hear that epigram spoken in the voice of revanchist exceptionalism, one that worships national power and prestige above all other values. And indeed, Patton's rhetoric about winners and losers has, over the years, been echoed in much of the best-known rhetoric about sports in America.

"Winning isn't everything; it's the only thing," legendary NFL coach Vince Lombardi said on various occasions. Lombardi actually stole this quote from its originator, UCLA coach Red Sanders. Lombardi did coin several original aphorisms in the same vein, such as "Show me a good loser and I'll show you a loser," which to this day are quoted approvingly by those who celebrate the cult of success, whether in sports, business, politics, or life.

There is no question that cult has played and continues to play a central role in American culture. But the cult of success continues to be opposed by a counterculture that, perhaps surprisingly, can be found, among other places, at the heart of the same sports world that often celebrates overtly authoritarian rhetoric. For on yet another level, sports themselves continually expose this same rhetoric as hollow, because it radically mischaracterizes what it means to take part in them, either as a player or a spectator.

Sports, like life itself, are always much more about failure than success. (George Orwell: "A man who gives a good account of himself is probably lying, since any life when viewed from the inside is simply a set of defeats.") In every competition, the number of losers vastly outnumbers the winners; this is especially true in American big-money team sports, whose tournament structure generally yields only one ultimate winner in any given year. (This is in contrast to soccer in other countries, which creates many subcategories of championships and other achievements that a team's fans can anticipate.)

Deeply engaged American fans know this all too well: indeed, to be deeply engaged is to recognize that one's engagement is far more likely to yield bitter disappointment than anything else. For the deeply engaged, triumphalism is merely obnoxious and in fact represents a travesty of the authentic fan experience, since it is nothing but a temporary reprieve from defeat.

When the Yankees were winning the pennant every year in the 1950s, Roger Angell remarked that rooting for them was like rooting for US Steel. (Both the dynastic Yankees and US Steel no longer really exist, as capitalism's famous gales of creative destruction tend to rip apart baseball franchises just as surely as they regularly wreck massive corporations.) This is why Yankee fans, like fans of the New England Patriots, or the Los Angeles Lakers, or Manchester United, or any other especially wealthy and successful team, are derided, or at least viewed with deep suspicion, by everyone else. Have these fans earned the right to enjoy the victories of their teams honestly—by suffering patiently through the bad times, which at least occasionally beset even the richest and most famous franchises? Or are they the equivalent of especially mercenary front runners in other social and political contexts, who associate themselves with successful enterprises only to the extent they remain successful?

In contrast to those deplorables who revel in the vulgar cult of success, fans of perpetually unsuccessful franchises wear the futility of their fandom like a badge of honor. That badge has bound together generations of fans of (relatively) lovable losers like the pre-2016 Chicago Cubs, the pre-2004 Boston Red Sox, and the present-day Cleveland Browns, as well as countless other franchises. Thus few things are more characteristic of deeply engaged fandom than the kind of competitive masochism that inevitably breaks out between supporters of even the most successful teams after a bad loss. And, by a kind of psychological thermodynamics of fandom, the more successful a team is, the worse any individual loss must be.

Whenever Michigan loses a football game—or for that matter during a game that the team seems at any risk of losing—the board, which a few hours earlier was full of sunnily optimistic talk, instantly gives itself over to a kind of mob mentality: it turns out that all but the most delusional observers realized all along that our players are inept, our coaches are clueless, and that everyone associated with the team is hopelessly incompetent or indifferent to our suffering or both. In the midst of this auto-da-fé, the rare voice of reason is shouted down furiously: yes, tomorrow is another day, but we don't want to hear about that now, immediately after our hopes have been dashed yet again.

The sharing of misery both intensifies and ultimately purges it, in a catharsis of collective grief: this is how we, the deeply engaged, take a sad song and make it better. Americans love a winner, of course—but the idea that we will not tolerate a loser is the kind of imbecilic claim characteristic of the more general stupidity that always marks author-itarian power worship in all its forms. (Jorge Luis Borges: "Dictator-ships foster oppression, dictatorships foster servitude, dictatorships foster cruelty; more abominable is the fact that they foster idiocy.") In fact, we more than tolerate losers; indeed the deeply engaged find ourselves bound more tightly to our teams by their most unforget-table losses than by even their most memorable triumphs.

For New York Giants fans of a certain age, nothing binds them together more powerfully than their memory of The Fumble of 1978. Although The Fumble refers to a single play (known to Philadelphia Eagles fans as The Miracle at the Meadowlands; like civil wars, these sorts of historical events tend to have at least two names) in an oth-erwise insignificant game played forty-three years ago, there seems little risk that this event will be lost to the mists of history, at least not any time soon. For one thing, at 6,721 words, the Wikipedia entry dedicated to chronicling The Fumble is approximately as long as the typical entry for an American president—and notably longer than the one chronicling the Giants' first Super Bowl victory eight years later. This rich text is the work of at least one deeply engaged Giants fan; more probably, like the Bible or the *Iliad,* it has multiple authors. The article goes into astonishingly obsessive detail, recounting every aspect of the circumstances before, during, and after the play, as well as describing the play itself with a level of granularity that would have impressed James Joyce.

The play is infamous because it is one of the most celebrated exam-ples of monumental coaching incompetence, snatching defeat from the jaws of victory and leaving the team's fans at first stunned and then utterly outraged. The situation was that the Giants had the lead and the ball with less than a minute left in the game, while the Eagles had no time outs remaining. This meant that New York merely had to fall on the ball to end the game. Inexplicably, the Giants' offensive coordinator Bob Gibson called for a handoff to running back Larry Csonka. Here is the climax of the Wikipedia authors' monograph:

> In the huddle, the Giants were incredulous when the call came in. "Don't give me the ball," begged Csonka. . . . Other players asked [quarterback

Joe] Pisarcik to change the play, but he demurred. Gibson had berated him for changing a play the week before and threatened to have him waived if he ever did so again. . . .

Csonka claims that, as he walked away from the huddle, he told Pisarcik he would not take the ball if he went through with it. It is not known whether the quarterback heard him or not, however. [Head coach John] McVay's headphones, which normally allowed him to communicate with Pisarcik and Gibson, were not working properly at that point either. McVay has since stated that he would certainly have overruled Gibson had he heard what was coming. . . .

The Giants wasted several seconds in the huddle in dismay over the play-calling. At the line, [Giants center Jim] Clack saw the play clock winding down and took it upon himself to snap it with 31 seconds left in the game to avoid a delay-of-game penalty, which would have stopped the clock and cost the Giants five yards. Had the Giants knelt on the subsequent play, there still would have been one second left on the game clock once the play clock ran down, requiring a fourth-down play to be run. . . .

Pisarcik, who at the time was distracted making sure Csonka was in position, was unprepared for the snap. It struck his middle finger so hard there was still blood on the nail after the game. Nevertheless, he held on to the ball after a slight bobble and tried to hand it off to Csonka. Instead, the ball hit Csonka's hip and came loose.

[Defensive back Herman] Edwards recovered it on its first bounce as Pisarcik unsuccessfully attempted to fall on it . . . [and] sprinted 26 yards untouched into the end zone for a 19–17 Eagles victory. There was stunned silence from the stands and the Giants' sideline. The only noise came from the celebrating Eagles.

This catastrophe triggered a full-scale rebellion among Giants fans, as hundreds publicly burned their tickets. A furniture dealer in New Jersey went so far as to pay for a plane to fly over the stadium during the team's next home game, pulling a banner reading "15 Years of Lousy Football—We've Had Enough." Gibson was fired just hours after the Philadelphia game and never worked in football again. Indeed for the remaining thirty-seven years of his life, he refused to discuss the play.

The Fumble gave birth to an entirely new standard play: the Victory Formation, in which a player is stationed 10 to 15 yards behind the line of scrimmage, in order to be in position to tackle a defender, should a similar disaster strike when a team is running out the clock. For Giants fans, the mere sight of the Victory Formation probably still elicits at least a subconscious shudder.

This compulsion to revisit the most painful moments of one's obsession is the essence of deeply engaged fandom. "Winning isn't everything; it's the only thing" is far less resonant to the deeply engaged than the words of the poet: "I am the man, I suffered, I was there."

That is the authentic voice of the fan. And it is, despite the claims of the authoritarian voices who bray about how losing is un-American, ultimately as American as baseball and apple pie.

LIVING YOUR GIMMICK

One way to appreciate the extent to which the often unhinged passions of sports fandom are seeping into other parts of our lives is to consider the various pseudosports that inhabit the psychological twilight world between fiction and real life, so-called.

For example, the Internet offers us a video of "The Battle of the Billionaires," a wrestling match that took place in April 2007 at Wrestle-Mania, the annual Super Bowl of professional wrestling. This event took place at Ford Field, the home of the NFL's Detroit Lions. The Battle of the Billionaires itself was a clash between wrestlers Umaga and Bobby Lashley, who had been chosen by Vince McMahon and Donald Trump to represent each of them in a proxy battle between the two plutocrats.

The backstory of this particular WrestleMania plotline was elaborate, even by the baroque standards of the campy and melodramatic pseudosport that is contemporary professional wrestling in America. That story begins three months earlier. McMahon, the undisputed tycoon of the "sport," arranges to have Rosie O'Donnell wrestle Donald Trump on McMahon's wild popular weekly USA Network telecast, *Monday Night Raw*. That match features wrestlers playing O'Donnell and Trump, rather than the real individuals, who at the time supposedly were engaged in a running feud in the media, no doubt concocted by their respective publicists. In the middle of the match, "O'Donnell" jumps out of the ring and gorges herself on a cake at ringside. Subtlety is generally not a feature of this particular art form.

Three weeks later, during an episode of *Monday Night Raw* in Dallas, McMahon appears in the ring as the impresario of what he is billing as Fan Appreciation night. McMahon begins by making fun of Texas accents and claiming that anyone in a cowboy hat looks stupid. Vociferous boos rain down from the crowd. McMahon, in wrestling argot, is playing the part of the heel—that is, the villain of the melodrama. He thanks the fans effusively for making him a billionaire. (This is not hyperbole. In 2020 McMahon's net worth was estimated to be $2.6 billion.) He then tells the crowd he wants to give each fan a special gift but can only honor one of them in this way. He "randomly" chooses an attractive and half-dressed young woman, who is brought into the ring and presented with an enormous facsimile of the cover of McMahon's magazine *Muscle Fitness*, featuring McMahon himself flexing his biceps. The boos become deafening.

At this point Donald Trump appears on the arena's giant scoreboard screen and upbraids McMahon for failing to give the audience "value" for their entertainment dollar, which Trump describes as his specialty. Trump says he is going to give the fans what they really want—money. (Wild cheers erupt.) Several thousand dollars in actual currency then rain down from the arena's upper reaches, triggering a frenzied scramble. Lucky fans display real hundred-dollar bills to the cameras for the millions watching at home. A supposedly humiliated McMahon starts ranting about how this is actually his money and demanding that the fans hand it over to him.

All this is what is known in the trade as "kayfabe." "Kayfabe" is the code word used traditionally by people in the wrestling business to describe those elements of the business that are presented to the audience as if they are spontaneous rather than scripted. Such elements include the conceit that the matches themselves are real athletic competitions, that the stage personas of the performers—their "gimmicks"—are something other than elaborate fictions, that the feuds, alliances, and romances between various performers in the ring and off stage are genuine, and so forth.

In our increasingly posttruth world, kayfabe can serve as a convenient shorthand for the whole genre of what in the broader entertainment business has become known as "scripted reality"—that is, scripted dramas that present themselves not as mimetic representations of life, like a play or a film, but as real-life events.

Professional wrestling is fake but represents itself to its audience as if it were real. This creates a complex mental state in much of the audience, hovering somewhere between, on the one hand, the willing suspension of disbelief in a dramatic fiction, and, on the other, the perception of what we take to be unscripted real-life events. People in the wrestling business refer to those taken in by any aspect of kayfabe as "marks." Fans who fully acknowledge that wrestling is nothing but kayfabe, yet who still revel in the drama as if it were real, call themselves "smart marks" or "smarks."

The McMahon-Trump kayfabe reached its climax after the two men signed a contract requiring them to each choose a champion to represent them in Detroit, with the stipulation that the plutocrat whose champion lost in the ring would then be shaved bald by the other. This was what was billed as the Battle of the Billionaires.

The highlight of the battle itself came when, in the midst of the contest, Trump himself attacked McMahon at ringside. The video of Trump—wearing, naturally, an expensive suit—running toward the similarly besuited McMahon, knocking him down, and then raining obviously fake punches down on his plutocratic rival's head, is must-viewing for anyone who retains even a shred of optimism about the future of our society. (Spoiler alert: nine years later, Donald Trump would be elected the forty-fifth president of the United States. In 2017, as part of his ongoing protofascistic campaign against "fake news," a.k.a. being subjected to criticism by journalists, Trump tweeted out a doctored video of his attack on McMahon, with a CNN logo superimposed on McMahon's head. A few months earlier Trump had appointed McMahon's wife Linda to his cabinet, as head of the Small Business Administration.)

Professional wrestling is one of the most culturally and economically important forms of reality television, and reality television itself has become one of the most characteristic aspects of twenty-first-century American culture. At bottom, reality television attempts to merge scripted drama with legitimately unscripted competition (i.e., the world traditionally dominated by actual sports). Most reality television involves a competition or pseudocompetition of some sort. That competition is then "managed"—sometimes partially and sometimes, as in the case of wrestling, completely—by a program's producers, in order to elicit the maximum amount of audience interest.

Over the past two decades, the remarkable popularity and resulting pervasiveness of reality television have combined to create various hybrid forms of sports, entertainment, and politics that blur the lines between these genres. Politics, and in particular political journalism, have been infected by these various hybrid forms of performance. It's true that political campaigns have long been treated by the media as if they were essentially traditional athletic contests, in which the entire significance of these events is reduced to their competitive outcomes, a.k.a. horse race coverage. It's also true that there is a long-standing tradition among political journalists of analyzing campaigns as if they were mimetic performances, to be judged in essentially aesthetic terms. This is sometimes referred to derisively as "theater criticism."

But the contemporary American political landscape is now also marked by a blending of genres, in which the mental states associated with viewing reality television, scripted reality, and professional wrestling—that is, genres in which what is "real" is presented in a deceptive or ambiguous way to the audience, while at least some of the audience is aware of this—have become commonplace. A related development is the increasing blurring of the lines between comedy and news, as in *The Daily Show*, *The Colbert Report*, and their numerous more recent spinoffs and imitators. Perhaps the most important original contributor to this genre was the satirical newspaper *The Onion*, which has straddled a line between parody and reality that becomes ever more tenuous. All these trends are amplified, of course, by Facebook, Twitter, and other social media.

Exhibit A of all this is the career of Donald Trump—a man whose supposed competitive triumphs in the quasi-sport of Who Wants to Be a Plutocrat were actually pure scripted reality. Trump inherited such an enormous fortune from his father—after first going bankrupt several times—that it's far from clear that he has as much money today as he would have if he had done nothing but passively invest

that inheritance. Trump's claim that he was a great high school baseball player who had a tryout with the San Francisco Giants on the
same day as future hall of famer Willie McCovey is among the most
bizarrely surreal of his many scripted tales about his imaginary accomplishments. Journalist Leander Schaerlaeckens dug up Trump's
high school baseball records and discovered he hit .138. And merely
glancing at a calendar reveals that Trump was eight years old when
McCovey was signed by the Giants.

Indeed Trump's entire career resembles nothing so much as the
classic trajectory of the heel in a long-running wrestling kayfabe.
The arrogant rich egomaniac is a classic wrestling character trope:
the most famous example is the Million Dollar Man, described by
wrestling aficionado Mike Edison as "the ultimate moneyed heel."
According to Edison, the Million Dollar Man "once offered a child
$500 if he could bounce a basketball fifteen times in a row, just to kick
the ball out from under him on the fourteenth bounce. He was lucky
to get out of the arena alive."

Trump is an absurdly cartoonish and preposterously melodramatic character, whose political success is possible only in a decadent political culture, within which politics have come to be treated
as some sort of particularly elaborate reality television show by both
a large portion of the audience and by the journalist-critics who help
create and maintain that culture. It's a culture in which the catharsis
offered by schadenfreude becomes, as in wrestling, the prime psychological and political value, and in which "kidding on the square"—
joking, but also meaning it—becomes as epidemic as it is on a pro
wrestling Internet forum.

In this regard, Trump is clearly "living his gimmick"—the phrase
people in the wrestling business use to describe a performer whose
ring persona ends up dominating the performer's life outside the ring,
to the point where the distinction between the gimmick and the person deteriorates or disappears altogether. After the 2020 presiden-
tial election, social critic and wrestling aficionado Jared Yates Sexton
pointed out that Trump and his enablers engaged in a "work"—
wrestling argot for a self-conscious fictional melodrama—by making
elaborate and facially ridiculous claims about how the election had

supposedly been rigged. But, as Sexton pointed out, "works" sometimes turn into "shoots"—the wrestling term for fabricated melodramas that the performers themselves end up forgetting are fabricated, because they've so thoroughly immersed themselves in the playing out of those fabrications.

It's increasingly difficult to remember that the man who succeeded Barack Obama as president of the United States was not very long ago a washed-up D-list celebrity, a running joke left over from the most deplorable aspects of the 1980s, who was peddling "Trump steaks" and flogging a flagrantly fraudulent "Trump University" to the most naïve and desperate marks. The implausible resurrection of Trump's cratered career was engineered by Mark Burnett, the Svengali behind *Survivor*, the most successful of the early reality TV shows. In 2002, Burnett rented an ice rink in Central Park to broadcast the live season finale of *Survivor*. The ice rink was leased by Trump, who naturally stuck his name all over it. As he took the stage to warm up the audience for the broadcast, Burnett noticed that Trump and the future Mrs. Melania Trump were sitting in the front row. Patrick Radden Keefe's *New Yorker* profile of Burnett describes what happened next: "I need to show respect to Mr. Trump, Burnett recounted. . . ." I said, 'Welcome, everybody, to *Trump* Wollman skating rink. The *Trump* Wollman skating rink is a fine facility, built by Mr. Donald *Trump*. Thank you, Mr. *Trump*. Because the *Trump* Wollman skating rink is the place we are tonight and we love being at the *Trump* Wollman skating rink, Mr. Trump, Trump, Trump, Trump, Trump.' As Burnett told the story, he had scarcely got offstage before Trump was shaking his hand, proclaiming, 'You're a genius!'"

Burnett had read his mark well. He soon signed Trump up to play the part of a savvy business tycoon on his new program, *The Apprentice*. This bit of kayfabe proved fabulously successful, despite its at-best extremely tenuous relationship to any reality found beyond the borders of a twenty-first-century American television screen.

Kwame Jackson, a contestant from the first season with a Harvard MBA, who had worked in private wealth management at Goldman Sachs with clients far richer than Trump, was not taken in by Burnett's carefully crafted illusion. He told Keefe he was "quietly amused when other contestants swooned over Trump's deal-making prowess or his elevated tastes—when they exclaimed, on tours of tacky Trump properties, 'Oh my God, this is so rich—this is, like, *really* rich!'"

Fran Lebowitz once remarked that Trump is "a poor person's idea of a rich person," and Jackson was struck by the extent to which Americans fell for the ruse. "Main Street America saw all those glittery things, the helicopter and the gold-plated sinks, and saw the most successful person in the universe," he recalled. "The people I knew in the world of high finance understood that it was all a joke."

Keefe notes that this was "an oddly common refrain among people involved in *The Apprentice*." Like smarks on a wrestling forum, they saw the show as pure camp. "The image of Trump as an avatar of prosperity was delivered with a wink." Yet "somehow, this interpretation eluded the audience." One of the show's editors was amazed: "People started taking it seriously!"

Did they ever.

One of the charms of competitive sports has always been that its dramas are unscripted. Fans rarely get Hollywood-style endings, which makes such endings, when they actually do occur, much more powerful than they are in a Hollywood movie. Reality TV, like any good capitalist enterprise, tries to eliminate the problem that real competition doesn't usually provide the most satisfying—and therefore profitable—story arcs. It gives us a fake version of reality, one that leaves out the many unsatisfactory elements of all true stories.

Professional wrestling is just an extreme version of this epidemic of unreality that has engulfed us. And Donald Trump's gimmick is just the most prominent of the many forms of kayfabe that have taken over our posttruth world. In that world, the lines between fantasy and reality are constantly being blurred by social forces that are turning everything from sports to politics into scripted melodramas, that generate immense profits and power for some, even as they degrade our culture and its most important institutions.

As the mental distortions of passionate fandom migrate from the sports world to other realms, even the most sophisticated smarks can end up having much more in common with the marks to whom they (we) imagine themselves to be so superior. To be a passionately engaged fan is to be, at least temporarily, something of an idiot, and forgetting that is precisely what allows the kayfabe of Trump and his countless epigoni to work its insidious magic.

WARRIOR-POETS

Just before the kickoff of every football game at Michigan Stadium, a so-called hype video plays on the enormous high-definition scoreboards. The presentation intersperses replays of moments of athletic triumph with glimpses of famous alumni and notable historical events—John F. Kennedy on the Michigan Union steps announcing the formation of the Peace Corps, etc.—and is narrated by the unforgettable voice of James Earl Jones, class of 1955. To describe Jones's voice as "resonant" would be like saying the Pacific has some water in it.

"This is the University of Michigan," the voice of Darth Vader and CNN intones, "where we respect integrity and honor excellence. We are loyal Wolverines, standing for midwestern values, hard work, determination, and an enthusiasm unknown to mankind [a charmingly nonsensical phrase employed by the current football coach, Jim Harbaugh, to describe how he attacks the challenges of his job]. . . . We bow to no man, we bow to no program, we are Michigan." As the video gradually whips the crowd into a frenzy, Jones reaches the climax of his peroration: "WE ARE THE BEST UNIVERSITY IN THE WORLD."

Every time I see the hype video, I cringe a little. It goes without saying that the best university in the world would surely not declare itself to be so. After an ankle-breaking, jaw-dropping 80-yard touchdown run, the great Detroit Lions running back Barry Sanders would simply flip the ball to the referee rather than engage in an onanistic frenzy of stylized self-congratulation. Act like you've been there before, as the saying goes.

Indeed, this entire ritual reminds me of the *Onion*'s brilliant (now two-decade-old) parody of the chauvinism of sports fans, "You Will Suffer Humiliation When the Sports Team from My Area Defeats the Sports Team from Your Area." A characteristic passage:

> One of the more pathetic aspects of the team from your area is the fact that only people in your immediate area possess an affinity for it. By means of contrast, the team from my area inspires loyalty and affection in individuals who live in many other geographic locations.
>
> To illustrate this point, let me tell a brief story: Recently, I was on vacation in an area of the country far away from my own, and I saw many individuals wearing items of clothing that bore the insignia of my team. I approached one such individual and asked him if he originated from my area. He said no, explaining that he simply liked the team from my area and had for many years. Interestingly enough, during this trip, I saw no clothing or other paraphernalia bearing the insignia of your team.

Anyone who has spent any extended time communicating with sports fans on the Internet has read claims very much like this many, many times. Mirroring the pursuit of saints' relics, people pay large sums for the facsimiles of the jerseys of great players, hoping perhaps that these totemic items can, by some mysterious alchemy, transmit some of the otherworldly powers of those players to their admirers. This constitutes a multibillion-dollar industry.

It also reminds me of a message posted by a Notre Dame football fan some years ago that in all seriousness (probably—it's the Internet, so one can never *quite* be sure) argued for the profound moral superiority of Notre Dame over the University of Michigan because of the former's commitment to objective moral values rather than secularized moral relativism, with this superiority being literally reflected by the light shining off the golden helmets worn by the school's players:

> On the surface, [Michigan's] football program appears to have much in common with the Blessed Mother's University's own. They are both ancient midwestern powers, at least by the temporal standards by which college football can be measured. Midwestern roots tend to flourish best

in the rugged soil of a punishing ground attack. Both schools are competitive universities, drawing a relatively similar student body, at least in the ways that the many measure such things.

But appearances can be deceiving:

The yawning chasm separating this bastion of hubris from the University of Notre Dame cannot be plumbed, even if one could measure the distance between the east and the west. At Notre Dame, the soul is gently nurtured in the understanding that all things seek but one ultimate Truth, that every endeavor under the sun only finds fullness to the degree that it furthers that pursuit. Excellence in all things becomes the goal prized by worthy and dignified creatures. They are obligated to pursue it in all they do, with all of their faculties. There is a unity in life, with a single focal point that will consummate every part, transforming them into living stones. Athletes are not merely athletes. Students are not merely students. All must share in the essential life of the school, never used simply as an object.

This is why my heart leaps every time I see Notre Dame's warrior-poets take the field, golden domes flashing in the sun. They embody the spirit of the agon, an all-encompassing pursuit of excellence alien to Ann Arbor, a wrestling with personal weakness to yield to transcendent strength. Her warriors are a visceral reminder of that very mystical body, every part dignified and fulfilled in its unique and blessed toil for the common good.

The reference to warrior-poets is probably an allusion to the ending of the film *Braveheart*: "They fought like warrior-poets. They fought like Scotsmen. And they won their freedom." The author probably did not intend to echo another film, *Apocalypse Now*, in which Dennis Hopper's character, a manic photojournalist, describes the deranged Colonel Kurtz as "a poet-warrior in the classic sense."

Now on one level, I'm engaging in what on what is known online as "nut-picking." Yet is this Notre Dame fan's wish to turn college football into a reflection of the eternal battle between the Holy Mother Church and the forces of secularism really any more absurd than the

University of Michigan's decision to employ one of its more famous alumni to make comically hubristic claims about the supposedly unparalleled virtues of the institution?

All of this is actually a reflection of how, over the course of the last generation, higher education in America has become obsessed with hierarchical sorting, in which universities are formally ranked against each other in the manner of football teams. Appropriately, the most influential of these rankings is that produced by *US News & World Report*, the electronic rump of a now-defunct print magazine, exercising zombie-like powers over colleges and universities. University rankings are a necessarily negative-sum competition for prestige and status, since the overall quantity of such positional goods is by definition stable. (In any year there can be exactly fifty top-fifty universities, etc.) This means the cost of competing to maintain or achieve such distinctions is, collectively speaking, equivalent to lighting that money on fire.

Ranking football teams has a certain twisted logic, since the whole point of the enterprise is competition for its own sake. Transplanting that logic to the realm of higher education, however, is preposterous to the point of insanity. This insanity is now culture-wide, however, as every obscure institution in flyover country spends untold sums advertising that it has just been certified as Number One—the national champion if you will—for online training in business leadership skills among small colleges in the Great Lakes region in 2022.

Thus does the culture of sports come to infest realms in which it is irrelevant at best, and more often actively harmful. And of course it's not merely higher education that's affected in this way; increasingly, the zealous partisanship of deeply engaged fandom gets carried over to other areas of life, particularly, but far from exclusively, contemporary politics. One of the Michigan board's longest-tenured and most active members is someone whose passion for Michigan football is matched only by his passion for the products of the Apple corporation, and he will not let any slight, real or perceived, to those products pass without unleashing an exhaustive demonstration of how wrong-headed such criticisms are.

I'm reminded of Orwell's definition of nationalism, in which fans of political entities identify themselves "with a single nation or other unit, placing it beyond good and evil and recognizing no other duty than that of advancing its interests." Such people, Orwell argues, are obsessed with securing "more power and more prestige," not for themselves, but for the nation or other unit in which they have chosen to sink their own individuality. Orwell is essentially describing fandom in the realm of the political cult: cult members support their team simply because it is theirs, and asking such people why they support their cult is, from the internal perspective of the group, likely to elicit as tautological an answer as asking Michigan football fans why they root for Michigan. In both cases, "because that's our team" is the correct answer.

In the realm of sports fandom, that answer is largely though not completely harmless; in other realms, it is often something else altogether. Sports teams and political parties function via a group psychology that is essentially the same, in which a kind of community is created through a shared rooting interest. In this light, while sports allegiances can be seen as a sublimated form of politics, political allegiances can also be understood as a form of sublimated fandom of the more traditional kind.

And, in an age marked by increasingly intense political tribalism, the basic psychology of sports fans in regard to their teams becomes increasingly germane to all aspects of political life. Historically speaking, this is a recurrent phenomenon: for example, 1,500 years ago, thousands of residents of Constantinople were killed, and approximately half the city was destroyed, in riots sparked by a conflict between the supporters of the Blues and the Greens, the city's two primary chariot-racing teams. Fandom has apparently been folly for a long time.

We should probably be at least a little disturbed that all five studio members of CBS's NFL pregame are required to wear a miniature American flag on the lapels of their suit jackets. Confusing rooting for the Patriots with rooting for the patriots cannot be healthy, especially in a culture where what exactly the latter kind of fandom ought to entail—what does it mean at present to be a "good" fan of the American project?—is a subject of fierce dispute.

We should also be disturbed by the extent to which schadenfreude—which is perhaps *the* defining emotion of fandom, especially online—

has also become the characteristic emotion of so many forms of political identity and affiliation. Nothing is more shamefully delicious than taking pleasure in the misfortune of the deeply engaged fans of your team's chief rivals, and indeed it's practically a formal ritual for some members of the board to visit the primary Michigan State, or Notre Dame, or Ohio State boards after those teams lose, in order to copy and paste the most agonized laments of our sporting enemies, for our community's amusement. (This psychological dynamic is captured perfectly by the title of Will Blythe's book *To Hate Like This Is to Be Happy Forever*, which is about the basketball rivalry between Duke and North Carolina. "The living and dying through one's allegiance to either Duke or Carolina is no less real for being enacted through play and fandom," Blythe points out.)

Their cries of anguish are of course essentially indistinguishable from ours on similar occasions—our players are inept, our coaches are idiots, the refs and the announcers hate our team, and so on (and on)—which only makes our vicarious reveling in that anguish all the more pleasurable. It's a twisted form of pleasure, but one that is considerably more insidious when it emigrates beyond the precincts of traditional fandom. Although schadenfreude can of course be found all across the political spectrum—many political blogs bear a striking resemblance to sports team fan sites—at present it seems to be the primary organizing principle of right-wing American political life, which manifests itself as an overwhelming desire to visit pain and suffering on liberals rather than any more constructive ideological goal. Thus the extent that schadenfreude is becoming the characteristic emotion of our age may suggest the extent to which the psychology of fandom—of placing one's team and one's affiliation with it beyond any introspective criticism—is affecting areas of life in which its influence is much less benign than it is in the world of sports.

Still, there are limits. Centrist complaints that politics have become too partisan and bitter overlook or ignore that, in an age of regenerate ethno-nationalism, authoritarianism, and even outright fascism, we really aren't all on the same team any more, in even the loosest sense. On the board, this became evident soon after the 2016 election, when a consensus developed fairly rapidly that open support of Donald Trump was not acceptable. Trump supporters were never banned as such, but any post supporting Trump would draw such ferocious responses that it soon became clear that their authors were considered by the community as a whole to be pariahs, and that if they wished to continue to participate in that community they would be best advised to keep their political fandom deeply closeted. As a result almost all open Trump supporters decamped to an alternative board, which predictably degenerated quickly into a cesspool of QAnon conspiracy theorizing and kidding-on-the-square racist invective.

Some things, in other words, can't be transcended by shared sports loyalties, nor should they. An Internet community that for twenty years had tolerated and even welcomed a broad range of political orientations, including traditional Republican conservatives, decided collectively, without any kind of formal process or coordination, that Trump-style authoritarian ethno-nationalism was simply too much. A number of lifelong Republicans still post regularly. They are either open never-Trumpers or keep their political opinions to themselves. This effect is certainly a form of, loosely speaking, censorship: specifically, the good kind. Support for authoritarian ethno-nationalism should not be tolerated, even on a Michigan sports board, any more than should the open white supremacy for which the alternative board now serves as the barest fig leaf.

All of which is to say that distinguishing between, on the one hand, the kind of malignant mindless fandom that places one's political commitments beyond introspective criticism, in the way one roots for Michigan against Ohio State without bothering to think about why, and, on the other, the principled rejection of political views and affiliations that shouldn't be tolerated, is not always an easy or pleasant thing to do. But that doesn't make doing so any less necessary, even as we laugh at the absurdity of hype videos and paeans to warrior-poets, while contemplating the partisan excesses of the age.

A SONG FOR YOU

For the first couple months of the epidemic, I pretty much accept that There Are No Sports. I occasionally surf through the sports channels, but I don't really watch anything. On the first of May I watch a minute or two of ESPN's now almost pointless *SportsCenter* and am informed that America has just endured its first April in 135 years with no major league baseball games. For some reason, this banal statistic seems especially plangent.

The past several weeks have of course been a programming nightmare for the ESPN "family of networks," as well as for another dozen channels whose standard fare consists primarily of live sports events. I mean, you have to be pretty far gone to watch the 1998 NBA all-star game or a replay of last year's Westminster dog show or the three-hundredth analysis of the NFL draft. The draft is pretty much the only "real"—for certain values of real—sporting event that takes place between mid-March and mid-May. I know I'm a junkie, but I'm not that much of a junkie.

But every man has got a breaking point, as General Corman informs Captain Willard in *Apocalypse Now*, and clearly I'm reaching mine.

Come Day 63 of the lockdown, I decide I'm going to watch some sports tonight no matter what. "No matter what" ends up meaning, initially, the 2015 NCAA lacrosse tournament semifinal between Denver and Notre Dame. My previous lifetime lacrosse viewing total had been under ten minutes. My preexisting knowledge of the sport consists of reading somewhere that it was a Native American game originally and that NFL legend Jim Brown was perhaps the greatest lacrosse player of all time, which I somehow find very easy to imagine.

I'm rooting against Notre Dame because it's Notre Dame and for Denver because the daughter of a former work friend of my wife's played for Denver's women's team. I watch about twenty minutes before the depressing realization that I'm watching a replay of a five-year-old game (match? contest? fixture?) that I know nothing about overwhelms the nascent interest that basically any competition elicits if I pay any attention to it.

Then it's on to something called The 2020 (Re)Open, on the Tennis Channel. This is a real live professional tennis tournament, featuring some real live professional players. The match I'm watching is between Reilly Opelka, a young American I saw play once or twice in the Before Time, and Miomir Kecmanović, a twenty-year-old Serbian, also in the top fifty in the ATP rankings, whose name doesn't really ring a bell but who, like Opelka, may turn out to be a superstar sometime in the future, if there is one.

This contest between world-class players is being played, appropriately enough I guess, at "a private residence" in West Palm Beach, Florida, on what looks like a backyard court, with no spectators, no linespeople (the chair umpire makes all the calls), and—somehow the most surreal touch—no ball boys or girls. Opelka and Kecmanović have to chase down their own balls after every point, like a couple of weekend hackers. The match is televised by a couple of cameras that hover above the chain link fence that surrounds the court, on what look like 40-foot booms. The skeleton broadcast crew actually does a fine job under these primitive conditions, and it's fascinating to watch the seven-foot-tall Opelka (the tallest player in ATP history) unleash massive serves from the idiosyncratic angles the cameras provide.

Finally I turn to the Big Ten Channel and watch, in an act of genuine desperation, about half an hour of an old Rutgers–Maryland football game. This is in the midst of what is billed as a marathon of great moments in Rutgers football history. Rutgers played Princeton in the very first college football game in 1869, which turned out to be pretty much the high point in Rutgers football history. I turn off Rutgers–Maryland, and for several minutes stare at the dark screen. I've recorded the first few episodes of *The Last Dance*, ESPN's series on Michael Jordan and the Chicago Bulls, but under the circumstances the title itself seems ominous. I decide to wait a little longer before turning to that particular fix.

For two months I've done OK without sports, or so I think, but now the yawning absence of my favorite waste of time is beginning to gnaw at my heart. My wife, who is much tougher than me in every respect, has no patience in general for my whining during the quarantine, and in particular on this subject. After all, she reminds me, tens of millions of Americans have lost their jobs, yet large sums of money keep getting deposited by my employer into our bank account, even though I barely have to do anything at my job now except teach a few classes via the suddenly ubiquitous Zoom technology.

"Read *Survival in Auschwitz*!" she upbraids me, when I wonder aloud how long it will be before I can go to a Michigan football game, or even watch one on TV. She has a point of course, but now, as I stare at the dark screen, which still retains the faintest glimmer of luminescence, I suddenly miss the old world—my world—with an aching pang of pure nostalgia. It's like the feeling one gets from coming unexpectedly, for the first time in many years, upon a once-beloved but somehow forgotten song.

> *Take me down to your dance floor*
> *I won't mind the people when they stare*
> *Paint a different color on your front door*
> *And tomorrow we may still be there.*
> "A SONG FOR YOU"
> GRAM PARSONS

BENDING THE KNEE

Within days after Derek Chauvin crushed the life out of George Floyd, an Internet meme was circulating: side-by-side photos of Chauvin kneeling on Floyd's neck and former San Francisco 49ers quarterback Colin Kaepernick kneeling during the national anthem to protest police brutality. The montage was labeled "Which Knee Bothers You More?"

Floyd's killing inspired such widespread horror and outrage that even some traditionally reactionary institutions started supporting the nationwide protests that followed. Ten days after the protests began, NFL commissioner Roger Goodell released an eighty-one-second video statement on behalf of the league. The statement was responding to requests from various star players, asking the NFL to condemn racism, and, more important, to admit the league had been wrong to fail to support the previous protests led by Kaepernick and to affirm that Black lives matter. Three-quarters of the league's players are Black.

Goodell repeated their words almost verbatim: "We, the National Football League, condemn racism and the systematic oppression of black people," he said. "We, the National Football League, admit we were wrong for not listening to NFL players earlier, and encourage all players to speak out and peacefully protest. We, the National Football League, believe that black lives matter."

Of course, Goodell and NFL owners don't actually think Black lives matter very much—this is a professional football league after all—but the sincerity or lack of it in the statement was almost irrelevant. What was important was that the powers that be in the nation's most high-profile and profitable sports enterprise didn't need a weatherman to tell them which way the wind was now blowing in regard to these issues.

Goodell's statement came on the heels of Drew Brees's remarkable about-face on this issue. Just two days earlier, the star quarterback said that he was opposed to the idea of players taking a knee to protest George Floyd's murder because he would "never agree with anyone disrespecting the flag of the United States of America." This statement provoked a backlash from many players, including his teammate and favorite receiver Michael Thomas, one of the leaders of the protests.

Within a day Brees had reversed his stance completely: "Through my ongoing conversations with friends, teammates, and leaders in the black community, I realize this is not an issue about the American flag. It never has been," Brees wrote on Instagram. "We can no longer use the flag to turn people away or distract them from the real issues that face our black communities. We did this back in 2017 [at the time of Kaepernick's initial protest], and regretfully I brought it back with my comments this week." Brees went on to say that "we must stop talking about the flag and shift our attention to the real issues of systemic racial injustice, economic oppression, police brutality, and judicial and prison reform. We are at a critical juncture in our nation's history! If not now, then when?"

Brees concluded by calling on his own white community "to listen and learn from the pain and suffering of our black communities. We must acknowledge the problems, identify the solutions, and then put this into action. The black community cannot do it alone. This will require all of us." Again, the key point here is not whether Brees's change of heart was wholly sincere, or driven in part by commercial and competitive considerations; the critical fact is that, almost overnight, Black Lives Matter had been transformed from a putatively radical movement into a mainstream position.

Brees's reversal infuriated Donald Trump, who for obvious reasons has long treated NFL players kneeling in protest during the national anthem as the sort of uppity failure to know their place that has stood in the way of making America great again: "OLD GLORY should be revered, cherished, and flown high," Trump ranted on Twitter. "We should be standing up straight and tall, ideally with a salute, or a hand on heart. There are other things you can protest, but not our Great American Flag—NO KNEELING!" In the days that followed, Trump returned to this theme repeatedly: he even claimed he wouldn't watch any NFL games if the league refused to require players to stand for the national anthem.

Sports were once again at the center of the culture wars—and the reaction of the sports world was providing powerful evidence regarding who was winning those wars. For example, when the PGA resumed play in mid-June, the tournament featured elaborate ceremonies honoring the memory of George Floyd and calling for racial justice. That the whitest, most politically conservative major sports organization in America was suddenly sounding like a college campus protest indicated the extent to which what had been derided as "politically correct" orthodoxy—that is, the claim that structural racism is at the center of American history, politics, economics, and culture—was with remarkable speed becoming a consensus view outside the most reactionary MAGA circles.

Naturally the inhabitants of those circles started bleating about how terrible it was that their beloved sports world was being contaminated by politics instead of remaining an apolitical sanctuary. One of the most preposterous outbreaks of such whining was emitted by Ben Shapiro, best known for his many tirades about how liberal PC snowflakes require safe spaces where they won't encounter opposing views. Shapiro was so outraged by the NFL's reaction to Floyd's murder that he claimed he was going to stop watching sports altogether, or at least until an apolitical league of some sort was provided for fans like him.

"My place of comfort has been removed from me," the anti–safe space crusader lamented. "It does make me wonder whether, inevitably, we are going to end up with two sports leagues—whether at some point people are going to want a sports league that does not allow this sort of [political] stuff to impede the play." Shapiro also complained that *Sports Illustrated* was forcing him to read about Caitlyn Jenner's transformation from Wheaties box Olympic icon to a representative of the struggles of transgender people. "What does this have to do with sports?" he asked, in all apparent seriousness.

People like Shapiro have no objection to the sorts of hyper-nationalistic rituals that are a routine part of NFL football games nor to the rampant commercialization that has led to the very fields the games are played on to be named after various corporate sponsors. Nationalism, militarism, consumer capitalism on steroids: none of that is "politics" to the Ben Shapiros out there. All that is just regular people saying and doing regular patriotic and profitable things in a totally normal way. Elaborate ceremonies featuring the national anthem are simply patriotic, which isn't political, while a player kneeling in protest during the anthem is unpatriotic, and therefore political.

But sports, like all socially significant activities, are always political: it's just that, if we remain sufficiently insouciant in our comfortably numb indifference to the political issues sports implicate, we can choose to ignore that fact. Since we are now living in what the Chinese curse calls "interesting times," that indifference is getting harder to maintain.

In the midst of the chaos of the Second World War, Orwell noted that "in our age there is no such thing as 'keeping out of politics.' All issues are political issues, and politics itself is a mass of lies, evasions, folly, hatred, and schizophrenia." In this respect, our own age is becoming more and more like Orwell's. Sports provide no refuge from that hard truth—nor should they.

THE MERIT MYTH

On October 12, 2019, Kenyan long-distance runner Eliud Kipchoge ran a marathon in 1:59:40, becoming the first person to cover the 26.2-mile distance in less than two hours. Those are merely figures on a page: grasping what they mean is actually rather difficult.

One of my favorite pieces of sports writing is an essay by David Foster Wallace, about professional tennis. Wallace himself was a very good high school tennis player—the best player in a several-county region—and in his mid-thirties he decided to go watch a professional tournament, with the vague idea of maybe hitting around with one of the less celebrated participants at some point.

He ended up centering the essay on a player named Michael Joyce, an obscure—by the standards of mainstream sports journalism—journeyman, at that time ranked just within the top one hundred players in the world. This meant that Joyce was someone who even most serious fans of professional tennis knew little or nothing about, assuming they had even heard of him at all. Joyce had to win several matches in a qualifying tournament just to get into the main draw of the tournament Wallace was covering.

Wallace asked readers to consider what this meant: "You are invited to try to imagine what it would be like to be among the hundred best in the world at something. At anything. I have tried to imagine; it's hard."

Eventually, Wallace comes to grips with what he now understands were his delusions about himself as a tennis player:

A child's world tends to be very small. If I'd been just a little bit better, an actual regional champion, I would have gotten to see that there were fourteen-year-olds in the United States playing a level of tennis unlike anything I knew about. . . . I still play—not competitively, but seriously—and I should confess that deep down inside, I still consider myself an extremely good tennis player, very hard to beat. Before coming to Montreal to watch Michael Joyce, I'd seen professional tennis only on television, which, as has been noted, does not give the viewer a very accurate picture of how good pros are. I thus further confess that I arrived in Montreal with some dim unconscious expectation that these professionals—at least the obscure ones, the nonstars—wouldn't be all that much better than I. I don't mean to imply that I'm insane: I was ready to concede that age, a nasty ankle injury in 1988, and a penchant for nicotine (and worse) meant that I wouldn't be able to compete physically with a young unhurt professional, but on TV (while eating junk and smoking), I'd seen pros whacking balls at each other that didn't look to be moving substantially faster than the balls I'd hit. In other words, I arrived at my first professional tournament with the pathetic deluded pride that attends ignorance. And I have been brought up sharply. I do not play and never have played even the same game as these qualifiers.

What Wallace discovered is that the gap between a very good tennis player such as himself and someone who can actually make a living, or even reasonably attempt to do so, as a professional in the game, was actually an immense, almost unimaginable chasm.

A striking real-life version of Wallace's aborted experiment took place in December 2019, when a local player decided to pay the entry fee to play in the first qualifying round of a low-level professional tournament in Doha, which he was able to do because not enough professional players entered to fill out a full field. He then proceeded to lose all 48 points in his match with the 1,365th-ranked player in the world.

One of the beauties of the sport of long-distance running is that you don't have to go to a professional event to understand exactly what elite runners are doing. You can understand it, to the extent it's understandable, just by putting on some running shoes and going down to your local high school track. A marathon is 26.2 miles, which is 42.2 kilometers. Your local high school track is 400 meters. To run a 1:59:40 marathon you would have to run all the way around that track in 68 seconds. And you would have to do that 105 times, consecutively and continuously.

It's actually very difficult to run 400 meters in 68 seconds—even most young athletic people will struggle to do that at an all-out sprint, and nobody can maintain a sprint for more than about 25 seconds, since the body will demand to slow down so that it can metabolize some oxygen. So Eliud Kipchoge ran 26.2 miles at a faster pace than the large majority of young athletic people can achieve for even a couple of dozen seconds. Another way of getting a sense of what this level of performance entails is to ride a bike with a speedometer and get it up to a bit more than 13 miles per hour. Imagine running that fast for two hours.

The same point can be made even more concisely at sprint distances. Every football fan knows that a 40-yard dash time of 5 seconds is very slow. It means a player isn't fast enough to play anything other than the offensive line or defensive tackle—positions on the field occupied by 300-pound-plus behemoths. A 5-second 40 time is so slow that plenty of fans are sure they can match it. Almost every one of them is wrong, as was demonstrated once by a Nashville radio station, which invited local weekend warriors to prove they could do it. Dozens showed up: exactly one of them achieved this feat, and he was a former college baseball player who had been the fastest player on his team. This means, among other things, that that "slow" 330-pound run-stuffing defensive tackle who looks like the Michelin Man can run faster than almost any football fan could have run on the fastest day of his life.

In one sense, competitive sports can be thought of as the closest things to a true meritocracy in societies, such as twenty-first-century America, that pride themselves on their supposedly meritocratic nature. This is because performance in these fields is generally both well-defined and objectively measurable: if you are genuinely excellent, it doesn't matter who your parents are, or where you went to school, or who you know, or if you seem "polished" in a job interview to someone who shares your tastes in food, music, films, etc. The reverse holds as well: it's very difficult to fake excellence in sports, as then-Speaker of the House Paul Ryan discovered when he claimed to have a personal best of "two [hours and] fifty-something [minutes]" in the marathon: it turned out his personal best was over four hours, in what was also the only marathon he had ever run in his life.

And it's probably not a coincidence that this is an area of American life in which people who have been discriminated against most ferociously in fields where performance is not so straightforwardly measurable have done exceptionally well. For example, the remarkable dominance of African Americans in professional football and basketball is no doubt due to many factors, but surely one of the most important has been that evaluations of what constitutes quality performance are much less subjective in sports than they are in almost any other part of our society.

This principle still has its limits: when I was a teenager in the 1970s there were no Black quarterbacks in the NFL. Coaches at every level of the game clearly believed, consciously or not—but often consciously enough, since they would say as much—that African Americans lacked, in the infamous words of Los Angeles Dodgers' general manager Al Campanis when he explained the absence of Black managers in baseball, the mental "necessities" to play the position.

So remarkable is the speed of human evolution and/or the ameliorative magic of the free market that today the NFL is full of Black quarterbacks, including several of the biggest stars at the position. We should also keep in mind that performing at an elite level in any activity requires, among other things, a fundamental belief in one's ability to do so. For example, the remarkable fact that, over the past twenty years, essentially all of the NBA's great white basketball players have been foreigners suggests that white American basketball players have been culturally discouraged from having that sort of belief in themselves. This in turn may be related to the effects of what psychologists call "stereotype threat," which occurs when people feel at risk of performing badly at something that their social group is stereotypically considered to be bad at. Perversely, the emotions elicited by stereotype threat then help produce the relatively bad performance that the stereotype predicts.

That sports resemble something approaching a true meritocracy is of course in many ways a good thing; but in other ways, the relatively meritocratic nature of sports has some insidious cultural effects. For one thing, consider what the economic structure of sports ends up looking like. In 2019, the top three men's tennis players in the world—Rafael Nadal, Novak Djokovic, and Roger Federer—between them made around $200 million in prize money and endorsement income. Meanwhile, the two-hundredth-best player in the world, at least in terms of earnings, Marc Polmans, barely made enough money to cover the considerable expenses of playing high-level professional tennis at all—such as travel, coaching, and, increasingly, support staff needed to be able to compete with the game's superelite.

Imagine, to echo David Foster Wallace, being the two-hundredth-best person in the world at something, with that "something" being a sport that generates billions of dollars of economic activity every year around the world, yet struggling to make enough money to make a living from that talent. The incredibly steep pyramid that is professional sports gives us a glimpse of what a true meritocracy—that is, one in which it is possible to determine with great precision who the top performers actually are—will end up looking like in any society that pursues it seriously. (It's almost never remembered today that the term "meritocracy" was coined as a pejorative by the British politician and sociologist Michael Dunlop Young more than sixty years ago.)

But the meritocratic nature of sports has a much more troubling social effect that goes far beyond the relatively tiny confines of something like professional tennis. After all, at any one time only a few thousand people are trying to make a living as professional tennis players. The bigger problem is that we as a society tend to transplant that meritocratic logic to other spheres, where a winner-take-all structure makes no sense whatsoever.

At the heart of the problem is the belief that talent is in short supply. Even in the world of sports, in which performance is much more narrowly defined and much easier to evaluate than in so-called real life, this belief is far more prevalent than it should be. More than thirty years ago, the iconoclastic analyst Bill James pointed out that the belief that in baseball talent is in short supply was a product of failing to grasp that, if baseball talent is normally distributed in the population as a whole, that means that the pool of potential major league players represents the very far right tail of that distribution. Players somewhere close to the major league replacement level will always greatly outnumber typical major league starters, let alone genuine stars. This in turn means that organizations that keep playing marginal or subreplacement players do so because of the mistaken belief that talent is in short supply, when in fact, at the replacement level, there will almost always be better options for creative organizations.

But the belief that talent is in short supply has far more pernicious effects outside the world of sports. Consider this revealing controversy from the summer of 2019. Jeffrey Goldberg, editor in chief of the *Atlantic*, gave an interview about gender imbalance at his magazine. The overwhelming majority of cover stories at the magazine under his editorship had been authored by men. Goldberg explained that, while he would love to showcase more women authors of long features, this was extremely difficult to do because the necessary talent was in short supply:

> It's really, really hard to write a 10,000-word cover story. There are not a lot of journalists in America who can do it. The journalists in America who do it are almost exclusively white males. . . . You can look at people and be like, well, your experience is writing 1,200-word pieces for the web and you're great at it, so good going!
>
> That's one way to approach it, but the other way to approach it is, huh, you're really good at this and you have a lot of potential and you're 33 and you're burning with ambition, and that's great, so let's put you on a deliberate pathway toward writing 10,000-word cover stories. It might not work. It often doesn't. But we have to be very deliberate and efficient about creating the space for more women to develop that particular journalistic muscle.

This is a classic statement of what could be called the merit myth, the essence of which is the belief that talent is in short supply. Goldberg's apparent belief that finding great women journalists is like finding the next LeBron James or Tom Brady or Mike Trout is—or should be—absurd on its face. It's not at all the same sort of thing, because, among other reasons, while there's pretty much only one way to hit a major league fastball, there are dozens if not hundreds of ways to write a great piece of journalism, and the ability to do so is therefore far more widely distributed in the population. (I have written a several-thousand-word piece for Goldberg's magazine, and I still say he couldn't be more wrong.)

As a practical matter, the merit myth exists to justify the maintenance of extremely hierarchical and antiegalitarian social structures. If there are ten or twenty or one hundred times as many people who have both the native ability and burning desire to, say, write cover stories for prestigious magazines, or to attend hyperelite colleges, or to be captains of industry, or to be good Supreme Court justices, or to star in a Hollywood movie, or to write the great American novel, as there are social slots available for people to fill those roles—and there are—then you've got to create sorting mechanisms that give the impression that those slots aren't being handed out arbitrarily, or worse yet on the basis of social privilege. What people want to believe is that occupying one of those slots—and most especially if they themselves happen to occupy one—is essentially like making an NFL or MLB or NBA roster.

Goldberg's mission, as he understands it, is to perform the extraordinarily difficult job of finding people who can write good cover stories for the *Atlantic*. He thinks this is hard because there so few such people. It *is* a hard job—but for exactly the opposite reason. There are enormous numbers of extremely gifted, hard-working, creative, and otherwise superbly qualified journalists out there, many of them working for nothing or something close to it, precisely because there are so many of them. This applies equally as much if not more to actors, novelists, aspiring disrupters of markets, potential Harvard-Yale-Princeton-Stanford, etc., undergraduates, and so on and so forth.

It's a big country. So what do we do? The answer so far has been a bunch of mostly phony metrics for sorting out sheep of supposedly unicorn-like rarity from the vast multitudes of putative goats. These metrics include things like whether somebody has a degree or preferably degrees from superelite educational institutions; whether somebody is related to somebody already in the business; whether someone seems, in the term used in Lauren Rivera's invaluable book *Pedigree: How Elite Students Get Elite Jobs,* "polished" enough and whether somebody knows somebody who knows somebody else who can vouch for them in an otherwise unnavigable sea of everybodies. The very week Goldberg gave his interview, the *Atlantic* itself published an excellent and horrifying story about the mad scramble among the parents of children already attending one of the nation's most prestigious private high schools to make sure their special snowflakes would have a leg up in the vicious fight to secure places at the very most elite and prestigious door-opening undergraduate institutions.

This kind of thing is inevitable in a society that talks itself into believing that "merit-based"—which of course ends up meaning to a significant extent class-based—decision-making is an adequate substitute for even the most minimal commitment to some sort of egalitarianism. And that's how you end up with the people currently at the top of various elite institutions believing that, like the general managers of professional sports franchises, they're performing some actual merit-based gatekeeping function, when in fact their real job is to perpetuate the existing social hierarchy, via conscious, semiconscious, and most often of all, conveniently unconscious self-replication.

VARSITY BLUES

In the fall of 2019, a small kerfuffle erupted when Justin Fields, the star quarterback for the OSU football team, indicated that, nearly a year after enrolling at the school, he hadn't really spent any time to speak of on campus.

It turned out that Fields was only taking online classes. "I can spend more time on football and studying, stuff like that," he told an OSU sports site. "Usually the assignments are all due on the same day, so that makes it easier for me." He added that he spent his spare time at home watching Netflix or at the Woody Hayes Athletic Center, where he took part in workouts and team meetings and enjoyed the various entertainment options available there. "But from what I have seen, the campus is beautiful, and the people around here are great," he added. The Woody Hayes Athletic Center features among many other things a lavish new lounge that provides busy student-athletes with made-to-order meals, massage chairs, video games on big screens, and a cryogenic chamber.

Shortly afterward, Fields's comments were echoed by LSU star quarterback Joe Burrow, who, after LSU's last regular season game, went over to the student section to celebrate. "I don't go to class. I take online classes so I don't get to see any of those people [LSU students]. And I kind of just wanted to see them for the first time and just thank them." Burrow had been enrolled as a student at LSU for seventeen months.

These comments from what would turn out to be two of the four starting quarterbacks in that season's college football playoffs led to much predictable tut-tutting about the apparently farcical nature of the "student" component of the student-athletes upon which this multibillion-dollar amateur sport depends. A subsequent AP survey revealed that, of forty-six major conference teams, twenty-seven had no limits on how many online classes athletes could take, and only six did not offer such classes.

The University of Michigan, not coincidentally, was the only public school among those six, with the other five being elite private schools. Michigan's football program has always taken considerable pride in how it supposedly holds itself to a higher standard of conduct than brazen football factories like LSU and Ohio State. And this attitude has become even more pronounced during Jim Harbaugh's coaching regime.

Harbaugh caused a stir that same fall when he was quoted in John Bacon's book *Overtime* as saying it was "hard to beat the cheaters." It's an open secret that many top college football and men's basketball players—the two sports that account for essentially all the money—are paid under the table in various ways, violating the NCAA's profound commitment to the sacred principle of amateurism. That is, the only people who should profit from the $9 billion of direct annual revenue these athletes currently generate (with indirect revenues probably more than doubling this figure) should be athletic department employees, NCAA and athletic conference executives, television networks, shoe companies, and myriad other associated enterprises.

Yet the economics of incredibly profitable enterprises being what they are, a vigorous black market for the services of the people whose labor actually generates those profits thrives and becomes ever more esoteric. Methods of payment now include, besides the traditional envelope full of cash, issuing players credit cards in other peoples' names, buying a player's family home for a sum well above its market value, and arranging for a player to get his old beat-up car repaired at a luxury dealership, which gives him a brand new "loaner" vehicle to drive until the repairs are completed, which will not be until his eligibility to play for Old State U expires.

All this horrifies those who think profit sharing fundamentally taints the purity of essence that ought to characterize the student-athlete experience. It frustrates these vestal virgins of the temple of amateurism to no end that, for the most part, the NCAA studiously looks the other way in regard to flagrant and ongoing violations of its rules. Their frustration is compounded by their appreciation of the fact that this selective blindness is a product of nothing more noble than the most craven self-interest: the president of the NCAA is paid more than $2 million per year, and he has an army of underlings drawing six-figure salaries from the firehose of income. In other words, it's best to let sleeping dogs lie, while the goose continues to lay golden eggs in a mostly unrocked boat. Still, that boat began to sway seriously in the summer of 2021, when the Supreme Court ruled unanimously that the NCAA's claims that it was exempt from various antitrust laws were legally indefensible. Almost immediately, the organization allowed college athletes to start licensing their names and images for profit.

Indeed, so pure are the hearts that beat in the labyrinth that is Michigan's Stephen M. Ross Athletic Conference—the name was bestowed recently, after a $100 million tax-deductible gift from the real estate developer's $7.7 billion fortune—that they long remained vigilant for signs the athletes who generate the money might be receiving any of it in any form other than company scrip, a.k.a. "athletic scholarships." Thus, in Bacon's book, Steve Connelly, Michigan's director of academic support, and Matt Dudek, director of recruiting (2019–20 salaries: $103,344 and $204,000 respectively) are appalled by the spectacle of those cheater southern schools finding ways to throw a little walking-around money to their players:

> It's also possible to "cheat legally." In 2015 the NCAA started allowing schools to pay student-athletes' "full cost of attendance," which includes travel, food, laundry, and other expenses not covered by scholarships which cover tuition, room, and board—a long overdue reform, praised by all sides of the equation. . . .
>
> Michigan's admissions office reported that, for out-of-state students, the "full cost of attendance" averaged an additional $2,400 per term.

After the NCAA rule passed, "because our school has integrity," Steve Connelly added, the figure remained the same. . . .

Meanwhile, . . . Alabama determined that their "full cost of attendance" for out-of-state students suddenly came to $5,386—or 34 percent more than they'd claimed the year before.

"You can't tell me," Connelly said, "that all of a sudden it became 34 percent more expensive to drive to Tuscaloosa." But Alabama's figure wasn't even the highest. Auburn claimed a bigger jump, to $5,586, while Tennessee calculated an additional $5,666 per term, the highest in the nation. . . .

"You can't tell me it's a coincidence that all three schools experienced a sudden spike in the actual cost of attendance," Connelly added. "You're giving these programs another advantage over our recruiters. Basically, those schools can give their players $3,000 more per semester than we do. Is it legal cheating? You tell me."

"Look," Dudek said, "we know there are people who don't operate on the same moral plane that not only Michigan expects, but coach Harbaugh demands. So the last thing I'm doing is going down that rabbit hole—probably be the fastest way to get fired around here."

Let's consider that precise "moral plane." The University of Michigan (2019–20 athletic operating budget: $196.3 million) could, while remaining perfectly within the NCAA's absurd and absurdly unjust rule structure, give an extra $5,000 per year to each of its football players, if it would just tweak its formula for determining the full cost of attendance. This would cost the school, basically, nothing—a few hundred thousand dollars per year—and it would give a group of young men who generate, conservatively, $200 million per year for the university a few hundred dollars per month in spending money, while at the same time helping the school's recruiting efforts against the "cheaters."

But no: Michigan, the leaders and the best as the fight song says, is just too special to allow itself to take any steps down this sordid path. The people who run the place—which has granted me three degrees, and for which I have the deepest affection—are so impossibly sanctimonious that they are affirmatively *proud* that they won't do something like this! Something, that is, that's within the rules, costs essentially nothing, makes a real difference to its beneficiaries—many who come from modest economic backgrounds—and also helps the program win.

But "we" won't do it because athletics isn't just about winning games: it's about building character, molding tomorrow's leaders (the Battle of Waterloo was won on the playing fields of Eton, etc.), and so on and on, ad nauseum. Meanwhile our head coach was getting paid more than all but four NFL head coaches, and there are approximately two hundred administrative drones in the athletic department pulling down six-figure salaries, including Connelly and Dudek. Why, bless their hearts, as the southern ladies say.

Bacon's book also makes much of how Michigan, unlike the football factories, plays things straight in terms of academics:

> "I think the word's gotten out to the recruits," Connelly said. "If you're not going to take academics seriously, you'll be better off going somewhere else." . . .
>
> "Our rules are simple here," Harbaugh told me. If a practice or a meeting conflicts with a class, we tell them to go to the class. They can't make up the practice, but they can make up the meeting.

This commitment to combining excellence in football with academic values does, however, run into a practical problem: there is no reason to think that the tiny slice of high school football players who are talented enough to play at a big-time program like Michigan overlaps much, if at all, with the pool of high school students who are academically talented enough to succeed at the highly selective academic institution that is home to that football program. The average Michigan freshman has an SAT score in the 96th percentile, along with something close to perfect high school grades. These attributes are very rare among talented high school football players, because they are very rare among high school students, period.

The university deals with this problem in two ways: by massively reducing entrance requirements for athletes and by giving those athletes all sorts of specialized academic help. There's an entire academic support center for athletes, which offers individualized tutoring and other resources. To what extent this kind of academic help morphs into something that could be considered academic fraud is difficult to determine. It clearly has at some institutions: a scandal at the University of North Carolina in the early 2010s revealed that some revenue-sport athletes were functionally illiterate, reading at a third-grade level or below. But, at least at Michigan, it "works" in the sense that it keeps athletes eligible and allows a lot of them to ultimately get degrees.

Now, it's inevitable that this sort of academic support system will competitively disadvantage schools that employ it. After all, a significant percentage of top football and basketball recruits have no interest in college as an academic enterprise or playing at a program that takes academics seriously. Some percentage of top recruits *would* be attracted to a program because it takes academics seriously, but this group is small. College football is now dominated by five or so programs that all the best players want to go to. (College football, like capitalism, naturally gravitates toward monopoly, absent strong regulatory intervention.) As part of their recruiting strategy, these programs barely pretend to enforce any academic standards, and they throw millions of dollars—legally, above the table—into lavish perks for players, such as ever more elaborate athletic centers, with massage chairs, giant video screens, etc.

In the existing postseason arrangement, the five or so currently dominant schools will tend to fill two or three of the playoff spots every year, leaving roughly another twenty pretenders, including Michigan, scrambling for one or two spots. (This also means there are one hundred or so major college programs that have no chance whatsoever of making the playoffs.) This is of course an extremely frustrating situation for the pretenders, who naturally complain about how the current elite programs cheat, by among other things not enforcing any academic standards. Contrast this situation with the NFL, which is basically a league of billionaire owners who try to maintain a microsociety resembling true communism: every single aspect of the sport is made as egalitarian as possible, in order to give every team a roughly equal chance of success. Thus it requires almost a miracle of sustained organizational incompetence—see the Detroit Lions and the Cleveland Browns for striking historical examples—not to win at least occasionally.

As someone who has spent almost his entire adult life in academia, I confess it amazes me that even some very intelligent people, who in other areas of life are not prone to sentimentality, delude themselves into thinking that the typical highly sought football recruit can actually do legitimate academic work at an even moderately selective university. The absurdity of this belief is evident if you simply flip it around: Is the typical student at such a university capable of playing college football? But in fact the analogy is more extreme than that: after all, superstar high school football players have more in common, in this regard, with the university's faculty, who were themselves academic superstars during their school days, rather than with ordinary college students.

What would a football team of academic superstars look like? What would happen if, for example, Stanley Fish, author of *Self-Consuming Artifacts*, and Judith Butler, best known for her *Gender Trouble: Feminism and the Subversion of Identity,* were your starting outside linebackers? Could these renowned scholars, with the intervention of, say, a special Athletic Support Center, be able to bench press 370 pounds or break 4.8 in the 40? I wouldn't be too optimistic about the prospects; still, this is roughly analogous to what the believers in the almost miraculous powers of "academic support" think can be accomplished.

Now, it's true that the typical undergrad at a reasonably selective college isn't any kind of academic superstar. Nevertheless, he or she is vastly more talented, academically, than the average high school senior—because precisely what it means for a college to be reasonably selective is that it admits students who are vastly more talented, academically, than the average high school student. And this remains true, to a somewhat lesser extent, at less selective universities. The votaries of big-time college athletics and the supporters of universal college education both refuse to acknowledge that most people can't do real college-level academic work any more than most people can play a competitive sport, at even a fairly low level of competition.

The notion that everyone can excel at academics is as obviously absurd as the notion that everyone can excel at sports. Big-time college football and basketball can exist only to the extent that this simple fact is ignored or denied. But because there are many billions of reasons per year to do so, that's what continues to happen.

Nevertheless, the current corruption of big-money college sports merely mirrors the corruption of their larger society. Consider the Varsity Blues scandal, which seized the nation's attention in the spring of 2019. This scandal revolved around various schemes used by rich people to get their children into elite universities via bribery. The traditional backdoor method is simply to give the institution a huge amount of money before little Jared's file reaches the admissions office. This method, though, has a couple of serious drawbacks. First, it cannot be structured as what Tammany Hall's George Plunkitt famously called "honest graft"—that is, there is still no guarantee that little Jared will actually get in. Second, even if it works, the whole world will know, or at least strongly suspect, what happened.

These inconveniences inspired an entrepreneurial fellow named Rick Singer to create what he called a "side door" to elite colleges. It involved bribing college coaches. Coaches at elite universities can essentially demand that the admissions office waive normal standards for athletic recruits. Almost everyone is aware that this happens in the revenue sports (football and men's basketball). What's not nearly as well known is that it happens in other sports as well, thus creating a very special kind of affirmative action. Caitlin Flanagan learned this as a college admissions counselor at a tony Los Angeles prep school:

> Legacy admissions have often been called affirmative action for white people, but the rich-kid sports—water polo, tennis, swimming, gymnastics, volleyball, and even (God help us all) sailing and actual polo—are the true affirmative action for the rich. . . . I was preparing for a meeting with the parents of a girl who was a strong but not dazzling student; the list her parents had submitted, however, consisted almost exclusively of Ivy League colleges. I brought her file in to my boss for guidance. She looked it over and . . . said, "Oh, she'll get in—volleyball."

Volleyball? Yale was going to let her in—above half a dozen much more academically qualified and many much more interesting kids on my roster—because she played *volleyball*?

But of course not everybody is good at sports, even fake rich white kid sports like sailing, polo, and fencing that exist at prep schools and elite colleges primarily to give those kids yet another leg up in the struggle to remain near the top of the "meritocracy," or at least not slide too precipitously downward. Singer's workaround for this was a masterpiece of simple mendacity: with college sports the broader public doesn't care about, you can just invent fake athletes, and no one outside the scheme is ever likely to notice. Thus the coach of the Yale women's soccer team accepted a $400,000 bribe to falsely identify an applicant as a recruit, while USC's associate athletic director and water polo coach received $1.2 million and $250,000 respectively to participate in a similar fraud. Stanford's sailing coach (good grief) took a $270,000 bribe to lie about the purported sailing prowess of two applicants. And so on. Singer would even photoshop the faces of applicants onto the bodies of actual athletes in the relevant—or more accurately irrelevant—sports.

My favorite twist on the Varsity Blues scandal took place, naturally, at Harvard, where a plutocrat bought the fencing coach's house for twice its assessed value. The plutocrat's son in fact had excellent credentials—top grades at St. Grottlesex and stratospheric test scores, plus the kid actually did fence—but hey, you can never be sure, so Daddy bribed the coach anyway. The scam would have gone undetected if not for the fact that a couple of house flippers noticed the otherwise inexplicable sales history of the property when the plutocrat turned around to sell it seventeen months later. They Googled the previous owner and joked that someone's kid must have wanted to get on the Harvard fencing team. A couple of weeks later the Varsity Blues scandal hit the media, and they decided to call the *Boston Globe*. This raises the question of how much of this kind of thing goes on without anybody ever noticing. My guess would be: a lot.

The Harvard administration was outraged to learn that Daddy was bribing a mere fencing coach, instead of doing things the right way

by donating a new building or endowing an academic center. The US Attorney, at the press conference revealing the Varsity Blues sting operation, actually said, "We're not talking about donating a building . . . we're talking about fraud." The school's reaction was reminiscent of the scene in Martin Scorsese's film *Casino* when the mob bosses discover that the guys in the count room have been skimming the skim. "We go through all this trouble and somebody's robbing us?" one of them complains bitterly.

So while it is undeniably true that college football and men's basketball corrupt academic standards at many institutions, those standards are being corrupted in countless other ways all the time, and for the same reason: the endless, insatiable need for ever more revenue that fuels every aspect of the decision-making process at these schools. Thus, academic standards have to be slashed—grade inflation now ensures that the traditional gentleman's C is now a B+—and not just for star football players but for countless children of the professional classes who aren't particularly academically minded but who nevertheless "have" to go anyway, both because college is a social sorting mechanism in this country and because higher education in America would collapse instantly if the only people who went to college were those genuinely interested in learning things.

The most notorious participants in Singer's scam were actress Lori Loughlin and her daughter Olivia Jade Giannulli, a nineteen-year-old "social influencer" with close to two million YouTube followers and more than one million Instagram fans. She had made it clear she had no real interest in actually going to the elite college to which she had been admitted—she was going only for "game days" and "partying." "I don't really care about school, as you guys all know," she pointed out. She did, however, provide a video tour of her dorm room and promised she would make more videos about life at USC (the twenty-second-highest ranked institution of higher learning in America, per the ubiquitous *US News* rankings): "I do have the opportunity to, since I'm in college now."

The combination of rage and schadenfreude that the Varsity Blues scandal elicited was understandable, given the increasingly severe bottleneck problem—there are vastly fewer places available at elite

universities than there are children who want desperately (or perhaps more accurately, whose parents desperately want them) to attend such institutions. Flanagan put her finger on why that response is often combined, especially among many white families from the professional classes, with intense feelings of entitlement, nostalgia, and resentment:

> They were experiencing the same response to a changing America that ultimately brought Donald Trump to office: white displacement and a revised social contract. The collapse of manufacturing jobs has been to poor whites what the elite college-admissions crunch has been to wealthy ones: a smaller and smaller slice of pie for people who were used to having the fattest piece of all.
>
> In the recent past . . . a white student from a professional-class or wealthy family who attended either a private high school or a public one in a prosperous school district was all but assured admission at a "good" college. It wasn't necessarily going to be Harvard or Yale, but it certainly might be Bowdoin or Northwestern. . . .
>
> These parents . . . are furious that what once belonged to them has been taken away, and they are driven mad with the need to reclaim it for their children. . . . They pay thousands and thousands of dollars for extended-time testing and private counselors; they scour lists of board members at colleges, looking for any possible connections; they pay for enhancing summer programs that only underscore their children's privilege. And—as poor whites did in the years leading up to 2016—they complain about it endlessly.

The Varsity Blues scandal illustrates, among other things, the incoherent way in which many Americans simultaneously embrace a naïve faith in the idea of a meritocracy and an often vague but still sincere commitment to egalitarianism. Everyone, we believe, should succeed—even though the system is structured around a mathematically absolute requirement that the vast majority of people must actually fail.

We recognize that fanning the dreams of poor kids to become the next Justin Fields or Joe Burrow is ultimately irresponsible, yet we

have no compunction about telling those kids that, if they work hard enough, they can get into Princeton or Stanford, when that is quite possibly even more unrealistic. The public agonizing by those who run such educational institutions about how to make them less elitist makes about as much sense as aristocrats puzzling over how to make their aristocracy less aristocratic. Elite educational institutions are by design carefully guarded class preserves, and they could cease to be so only if they became completely different sorts of places.

All this can lead to sanctimony and cynicism. In the former category, we have Michigan's athletic department, which imagines that its football team is a peer of Ohio State, while its university is a peer of Stanford. At present it would be difficult to say which belief is more delusional. Among believers in the latter, we have everyone who dismisses the department's professed idealism as nothing but brazen self-conscious grifting. I am sufficiently uncynical to believe this particular variety of grifting remains mostly unconscious.

Avoiding either sanctimony or cynicism is, under the circumstances, not easy. But it is possible to value and even love something one knows to be deeply corrupt while trying to make it less so. Indeed, in America at present, that might be the essence of patriotism.

AFTER THE GOLD RUSH

The long feature story in the nation's leading sports magazine paints a grim picture. The economic structure of college athletics is now completely out of control: even the top programs find it increasingly difficult to pay their bills, as costs soar, and revenue growth is stalled by intense competition for the entertainment dollar. Even the University of Michigan's athletic department—the highest-grossing enterprise in the business—is beginning to feel the pinch. Given the current crisis, the author poses a stark question: Can big-time college athletics survive? Michigan's athletic director has a plan. He, the article says, "peddles 'enjoyment' as he once peddled socks, and has little trouble footing Michigan's whopping bill."

This four-thousand-word *Sports Illustrated* feature on Don Canham was published in the summer of 1975. It relates that, in the following year, "the University of Michigan will have an athletic budget of $4.5 million, more than twice what it was when Canham took over" in 1968. Because of spiraling costs, Canham says, the modern athletic director has to "hustle like a whore on Main Street." For his efforts, the university pays Canham a salary of $38,000—one of the of the highest salaries of any athletic director in the country.

Translated into 2021 dollars, that budget was equivalent to $21 million, while Canham's salary equates to $176,000. And it's safe to say that big-time college athletics have in fact survived, at least so far. For instance, that same athletic department is generating, in fiscal 2020, $196.3 million in revenue, which not coincidentally happens

to be exactly the sum the department is spending. Canham's most recent successor, Warde Manuel, is in the middle of a five-year contract
worth nearly $5 million. Manuel's compensation, however, currently
doesn't even rank in the top twenty for college athletic directors.
Jack Swarbrick at Notre Dame received more than $3 million in 2018.

My history with the institution ensures that I will never be overlooked when the University of Michigan is soliciting funds. Thus after
the Victors for Michigan campaign kicked off in 2013, I was bombarded with requests to help the university reach its $4 billion goal.
"Be a Victor for Michigan Law Today" read a typical solicitation. I
eventually donated a modest sum, partially out of sentiment—"The
Victors" is the school's fight song, and the fundraisers obviously
knew their target audience well—and partially out of a desire to get
them to stop.

The campaign was a smashing success, raising a total of $5.28 bil-
lion. The demographics of the nearly four hundred thousand donations to it are revealing. Ninety-four percent of those donors gave less
than $5,000. If we assume, optimistically, that the mean donation
among such donors was $1,000—it was surely much lower—then
we 94 percenters accounted for approximately 7 percent of the total
donations. That would mean the average donation among the top
6 percent of donors, who collectively accounted for 93 percent of
the money, was just over $200,000. This public institution's fundrais-
ing is for all practical purposes completely dependent on the favor
of a relative handful of very rich people, while the donations of the
overwhelming majority of contributors end up being essentially faux-
democratic window dressing.

I thought of this relationship in August of 2019, when I read that
Stephen Ross, a multibillionaire who owns the NFL's Miami Dol-
phins, was holding a $250,000 per plate fundraising dinner for Don-
ald Trump, at Ross's Long Island estate. Besides dinner, that sum
bought donors a "private roundtable" meeting with the president
of the United States. Ross is the nephew of Max Fisher, a fabulously
successful Detroit-area businessman who founded a chain of gas
stations, which he sold to Marathon Oil in 1959 for $40 million—
equivalent to $355 million today. So Ross didn't exactly pull himself

up by his bootstraps or anything, but he did parlay a (relatively) modest family loan into a $7.7 billion fortune.

Ross has lavished some of his wealth on his alma mater: he donated $150 million to Michigan's business school in exchange for having it named after him, and another $100 million to the athletic department in exchange for having his name grace the athletic campus. (It's worth noting that $250 million is all of 3.2 percent of $7.7 billion.) One of the key factors that has made the New Gilded Age possible is that human beings are generally quite bad at math. For example, consider the following thought experiment: If an ATM spit out one dollar bill every second, how long would you have to stand in front of it to collect one million? The answer is eleven and a half days. How long would you have to stand in front of it to collect one billion? Almost thirty-two years. Now how long would you have to stand in front of it to be as rich as Jeff Bezos? The answer is 6,340 years.

Ross's aggressive fundraising for Trump caused something of an outcry among various Michigan students, faculty, and alumni, many of whom did not like the idea of the name of one of Trump's most prominent plutocratic supporters being plastered all over their campus. Some even demanded that the institution give Ross back his money, which, given the economic and ideological structure of the contemporary university, might as well have been a demand to suspend the laws of thermodynamics. Ross was taken aback by these criticisms, and so he made it known that, while he liked Donald Trump's tax breaks for billionaires, that did not mean he approved of Trump's ethno-nationalist white supremacy program:

> Although Ross supports Trump's re-election efforts and the two have been personal friends for decades, a source close to the Dolphins owner and wealthy New York real estate developer says Ross does not support Trump's views regarding race.
>
> "They agree on some things and disagree on others, specifically on the rhetoric around race," the source told the *South Florida Sun Sentinel*. "With regards to race, Stephen's record on fighting racism speaks for itself. It is possible to support someone on the basis of some things, and not agree with everything about them."

If my contribution to fighting racism included doing everything I could to get Donald Trump re-elected, I think I would keep that whole "fighting racism" section off my resume. In the end, Ross is just another plutocrat who is willing to put up with a little, or actually a lot, of white supremacy, in exchange for some sweet tax cuts.

(Again, our inability to do math is of immense value to the plutocracy. In a 2014 interview, the comedian Chris Rock was asked about how little sense there still is among ordinary Americans regarding the immense gaps in basic life experiences created by the class system. "Oh people don't even know," Rock replied. "If poor people knew how rich rich people are, there would be riots in the streets. If the average person could see the Virgin Airlines first-class lounge, they'd go, 'What? What? This is food, and it's free, and they . . . what? Massages? Are you kidding me?'" It's increasingly the case that one of the privileges of being rich is that you don't have to pay for anything.)

In any case, the extent to which America's public universities are being quasi-privatized is one of the most striking and least talked about aspects of the New Gilded Age. Part of this of course is a consequence of cuts in state funding, which nationally has declined by about 15 percent per student since its peak in the late 1980s and has declined far more drastically as a percentage of national GDP. The situation is more extreme in Michigan, where the economy has probably done worse, relatively speaking, than in any other state over the past half century. Indeed, in 2019 the University of Michigan's state appropriation was 20 percent lower, in real dollars, than it was in 1966, when the national per capita GDP was 40 percent of what it is today.

Still, to a significant extent, state funding cuts have just provided a handy excuse for a radical level of corporatization and quasi-privatization that these institutions were and are all too eager to embrace anyway. If you think you're running a multibillion-dollar business, rather than an institution that was set up to be in many ways the opposite of a business, it suddenly becomes much easier to pay your top administrators as if they were C-suite executives, because "the market" in its mysterious wisdom now positively demands that you do so, just as it does in the corporate world.

Nothing illustrates this economic and ideological shift better than the growth in elite public university endowments. When I received my undergraduate degree from Michigan in 1982, the university's endowment was $115.3 million ($326 million in 2021 dollars). By the summer of 2021 that endowment had grown to $17 billion—an astonishing *fifty-two-fold* increase in real, inflation-adjusted dollars. Note that, a generation ago, significant endowments simply didn't exist at public universities—with the exception of those in Texas, into which the legislature funneled oil money—and indeed could be found at only about a dozen hyperelite private schools. Now, more than one hundred schools have endowments of over $1 billion.

This is almost entirely a result of two factors: a lot of extremely rich people have given enormous amounts of money to the school, and the financial markets that have made those extremely rich people extremely rich have boomed over the course of the New Gilded Age. (We also shouldn't overlook that, in the case of donations to entities like universities, those donations are subsidized heavily by the American taxpayer, because they are deductible.) It's hardly surprising that, despite the delusions of right-wing critics that elite universities are hives of left-wing indoctrination, our contemporary plutocracy has in fact found invaluable support emanating from institutions of higher learning that have learned gradually, one way or another, to sing for their supper.

Thus it is that the University of Michigan, one of the nation's great public institutions of higher education, has transformed itself into a "public ivy," by prostrating itself constantly before that plutocracy and servicing, consciously or unconsciously, its fondest desires. The problems with this should be obvious, but so purblind has our worship of The Market become that the purchase of the intellectual patrimony of the nation by a bunch of obscenely rich narcissists is treated as an unambiguously blessed event, as opposed to a version of another kind of transaction you might witness every night on a seedy side street, if you're inclined to look at what's actually going on.

And all of this pervasive money madness has endless insidious ripple effects. Once a social system has moved all or nearly all of its members above the level of brute starvation, wealth, and poverty soon become relative concepts—but that doesn't make them any less real. Thus one of the consequences of living in an extremely rich country which features increasingly extreme wealth stratification is that people who would until very recently have been considered simply rich are suddenly part of the anxious "upper middle class."

In the contemporary American university, the effects of this sort of relative immiseration are particularly striking. For example, Lee Bollinger, who was a full professor at Michigan's law school when I was an undergraduate in the early 1980s, was at the time being paid $31,500 for his services—a little more than $100,000 in 2021 money. The university's president, Harold Shapiro, earned $75,000 ($220,000 in 2021 dollars). Bollinger is now the president of Columbia, where he is paid a hair under $4 million per year. On the other hand, he's paid nearly $3 million *less* than the guy who runs Columbia's $11 billion endowment. (More than eighty university presidents had seven-figure salaries in 2018.)

Nevertheless I wouldn't be surprised if Lee Bollinger doesn't feel rich, despite the fact that he makes, in real, inflation-adjusted terms, more money every two weeks than he did in an entire year when he was a full professor at an elite law school. After all Bollinger's job consists largely, as a matter of cruel financial necessity, of attempting to wheedle money out of people who themselves earn more in two weeks than he now makes in a year. Relatedly, the fact that the football coach at Michigan makes $7.5 million per year makes it easier for Michigan to pay literally dozens of administrators more, in real, inflation-adjusted terms, than what President Shapiro was making when I was an undergraduate.

When Bo Schembechler became Michigan's head football coach in 1969, his salary was $144,000 *in 2021 dollars*. Twelve years later, that salary had just about doubled in real terms (Schembechler had at the time the highest winning percentage of any college football coach.) Then Texas A&M, awash in oil boom money, decided to offer a 139 percent raise to the equivalent to $680,000 in 2021 dollars. Michigan beneficiary and pizza magnate Tom Monaghan gifted Schembechler one of his franchises—located in Columbus, Ohio, home of Ohio State University, in a nice example of what today would be called trolling—and Schembechler turned TAMU down.

In 2019, Michigan's current coach, Jim Harbaugh, was paid $7.5 million in direct compensation, not including all sorts of fringe benefits, such as free cars and private jet travel. Harbaugh is not close to being the highest-paid college football coach, either. That year that distinction went to Clemson's Dabo Swinney, a Christian gentleman much offended by the very notion of paying college football players, who was paid $9.3 million, not including incentives. If Clemson were to win the national championship in any season—something the team had done in two of the three previous years—Swinney would receive an additional $1.125 million in pay. He also got two new cars every year, country club memberships, free travel for his family to away games, and so forth. The following year Alabama's Nick Saban received $9.75 million for his services.

Big-time college athletic department budgets, and the compensation for their highest-paid employees, have increased by a factor of more than ten in real dollars, since the days when it was said that college athletics were on the verge of bankruptcy. Where is this tsunami of dollars coming from? One source is those same extremely wealthy people filling the coffers of the fundraising campaigns. Thus it has come to pass that, in 2021, Michigan doesn't just have a head football coach: Harbaugh is, officially, the J. Ira and Nicki Harris Family Head Football Coach, while defensive coordinator Mike Macdonald is the Lester Family Defensive Coordinator, and offensive coordinator Josh Gattis is the Sanford Robertson Offensive Coordinator. That assistant positions now have their own independent endowments to help fund these crucial aspects of the institution's educational mission is symptomatic of the extent to which everything in our society is gradually being put up for sale, while at the same time being turned into an advertisement to sell something else.

Another source is the cost of tickets to games, which has recently gone through the roof at all big-money programs. For the first three decades of my fandom, ticket prices for Michigan football games were stable in real dollars: from 1971, when I attended my first game, until the late 1990s, a full-price ticket cost about $40 in 2021 dollars, and a student ticket cost half that. Indeed, in constant dollars, ticket prices had remained largely unchanged since the 1940s.

Then, almost overnight, the situation changed dramatically. The big jump came in 2005, when Michigan joined the private seat-license racket—referred to demurely by administrators as "Preferred Seat Donations." Suddenly, in order to buy season tickets, fans had to pay not just for the tickets but for the right to purchase them. For example, in order to purchase a moderately priced season ticket at the 20-yard line, a fan has to pay not only the $550 face value but an additional $525 in the form of a PSD. The season tickets are for seven individual games, so the per-game cost totals $154—a rough quadrupling of the real price of tickets that obtained from the 1940s through the 1990s.

And it's possible to pay far more than this: the PSD for the luxury suites—excuse me, for what university administrators have dubbed "enclosed premium seating"—which were added to Michigan Stadium in 2008, varies from $60,000 to $90,000 per season. Again, this figure doesn't include the tickets themselves. Since sixteen tickets are available per game per suite, the average real price of a single game suite ticket is a very reasonable $741, assuming the purchaser has $83,800 handy to rent the suite for the season, plus parking and concessions.

What was once the essentially democratic and even vaguely socialistic experience of attending a Michigan football game—all the tickets were the same fairly low price, and everyone sat, wedged together, on the same uncomfortable metal bleachers—has been transformed into yet another plutocratic spectacle, at which the privilege to attend is parceled out at prices that range from the moderately exorbitant to the completely obscene, with the groundlings shivering in the end zone, while the Lords of Capital hover high above in their climate-controlled suites, contemporary aristocrats heedless of any potential revolt.

My favorite detail of this New Gilded Age tableau is that, until 2019, 80 percent of the PSD was deductible as a donation to the university, which, legally speaking, is a charity. And, when the PSDs became nondeductible last year, the athletic department raised the cost of them anyway, explaining that the $30 million generated by PSDs—in real dollars a sum 50 percent larger than the entire budget of the nation's largest athletic department in the mid-1970s—"allows Michigan Athletics to remain one of the few self-sustaining athletic departments in the country." (This is reminiscent of how university administrators love to explain that the reason tuition is going up is because costs are rising, when the reality is more or less exactly the reverse: costs are rising because tuition is going up.)

Yet despite this massive increase in ticket revenue, the majority of the new money that has flowed into big-time college sports over the last few decades has another source: television. In the early 1970s, ABC was paying a total of $12 million per year (about $80 million in 2021 dollars) for the exclusive right to televise regular season college football games. In fiscal 2019, major college sports programs received more than $2.5 billion in television revenue distributions from their respective conferences—that is, more than a thirty-fold increase over what these programs were receiving when *Sports Illustrated* was first bemoaning the money madness of college sports. The biggest individual source of this revenue was ESPN, the Disney-owned sports channel behemoth, which has paid several billion dollars for the right to broadcast college football over the course of the last few years. ESPN, in turn, can pay these enormous fees because of the wildly inefficient economic structure of cable and satellite television. ESPN received $7.3 billion from subscribers in 2018, as each paid about nine dollars per month to receive the "ESPN family of networks." With eighty-five million such subscribers, that adds up to real money. But here's a remarkable fact: *70 percent of those subscribers never watch ESPN!*

Under the traditional pricing structure of pay TV, people can't subscribe to a cable or satellite service without paying for ESPN, which is included in the base channel package for all subscribers. Thus, the large majority of ESPN's revenue is coming from people who don't want what they're paying for. This, needless to say, isn't a particularly sustainable situation; and the fact that "cord cutting" has reduced ESPN's total subscribers by around 20 percent over the course of the last decade suggests its end is nearing.

But for now, at least, the money machine rolls on. This is both because deeply engaged fans will pay a great deal of money for their fix, and because the shallow engagement of the casual fan also generates a lot of revenue. As someone who has lived his life inside both categories for decades, I'm well aware of how that machine gets fueled. For one thing, because I want to watch sports on TV, I've paid something like $15,000 in satellite subscription fees over the past decade alone—a figure that fills me with equal parts of amazement and dread as I glance at the back of this metaphorical envelope. For another, I've paid a sum I don't even want to calculate to attend Michigan football games, which I continue to do every year, even though doing so requires a thousand-mile plane flight for starters. And I waste—or perhaps "waste"—literally thousands of hours per year on the Internet following Michigan football: hours that could be, as the economists say, "monetized" in the pursuit of lucrative and perhaps even socially useful work.

And all that, sadly, is the tip of the proverbial iceberg. A huge amount of the sports on TV are on TV in large part because people like me will watch almost any sort of garbage. I'll watch, for instance, a late-night replay of a second-division English soccer match, at least for a while, between two teams that I've never heard of, because it's sports and it's on. Beyond that, I'm aware that people in Brentford and Swansea are living and dying with each twist and turn of the action, and, if I get one tenth of 1 percent of the rush they're getting via the most attenuated form of proxy fandom, that's still better than watching *House Hunters International*, probably.

Ultimately, the economics of big-time sports in America are, for anyone who has even the most mildly progressive political commitments, not really defensible. Every time I watch the *Toyota Halftime Show* from AT&T Stadium ($325 million of the cost of building this sybaritic playpen for Dallas Cowboys owner Jerry Jones—net worth, $4.2 billion—came straight out of taxpayers' pockets), I'm reminded of how grotesque so many aspects of the money side of this thing of ours really is. Ultimately, to have been sports fans over the past few decades is to have witnessed how our passions have been identified, cataloged, and then exploited by the relentless engines of hypercapitalism, in its insatiable pursuit of ever-greater profits.

Can things go on like this forever? Obviously not: as the famous economist Herbert Stein once noted, if something cannot go on forever, it will stop. When that will be is anyone's guess. After all, when my son reaches my present age, it's possible that these speculations will seem as unduly pessimistic as *Sports Illustrated*'s were in 1975, and that Michigan's head coach will by then be collecting a $75 million salary, as part of the athletic department's $2 billion operating budget. Nevertheless, in the truly long run, it's surely the case that the ever-accelerating money machine will exceed tolerable limits, and the whole thing will come crashing down, in one way or another.

That observation, however, brings to mind the dictum of an even more famous economist—John Maynard Keynes—that in the long run we're all dead. And in the meantime the band plays on.

ONWARD CHRISTIAN SOLDIERS

If a modern-day Tocqueville were to travel through America, seeking enlightenment regarding the nature of this mysterious country, he could do worse than to visit the football practice field at Clemson University, in the heart of the football-crazed Old Confederacy. If he had passed through on a certain day in August of 2012, he would have witnessed the football team's coach, Dabo Swinney, calling the team together at the end of practice for some final remarks. Swinney announced to the team that star wide receiver DeAndre Hopkins—later one of the NFL's best players—was about to be baptized on the field. Swinney invited all the team's players and coaches to stay and watch.

Apparently, everyone did. The team gathered around the kind of immersion tub that is normally used by players taking an ice bath after practice. It was filled with water, and Hopkins climbed into it, still wearing his uniform and shoulder pads. "Jesus is the most important thing in my life," he told his coaches and teammates, "and I want you guys to know I'm living for him." A pastor from NewSpring, a local Baptist church, then proceeded to perform the baptism, to the cheers of the team.

An assistant coach was moved sufficiently by the proceedings to snap a photo of it, which later came to the media's attention. Clemson is a public university, so holding an actual baptism at what for the student-athletes on the team is a mandatory school event is an egregious violation of modern First Amendment law, which holds that public institutions cannot promote or endorse religion.

In 2014, a nonprofit organization filed a complaint, asking Clemson's administration to stop any further such behavior on Swinney's part, including such practices as team prayers, Bible study sessions, and organized church trips that the coach had made an integral part of the football program. University administrators said they would look into it. Five years later, in the fall of 2019, they were apparently still looking into it, as Swinney's on-the-job evangelizing continued unabated.

Dabo Swinney claims to love Jesus a whole lot, and he certainly wins a whole lot of football games. Those two achievements make him, in contemporary Red State America, pretty much invulnerable to administrative or any other sort of sanction.

To get some perspective on what has happened to America's economic structure in general, and that of American universities in particular, we can look back nearly forty years, to an article published in the *New York Times* in 1982, regarding Jackie Sherrill's new contract to coach the Texas A&M football team.

The article's author, Gordon White, clearly intends to convey, within the prim constraints of "objective" journalism, a sense of shock and disbelief that Sherrill is going to be paid the staggering sum of $280,000 per year to coach a college football team. The very idea that a university, of all things, would pay an employee $280,000 per year is presented implicitly as outrageous: "According to the best estimates of several officials with a broad knowledge of higher-education matters," White writes, "no other person has ever received so much in pay from an American university."

This seems plausible: for example, a broad-based 1983 study of the compensation of American university presidents found a mean compensation of $63,501, with no president making more than $118,000. (Apparently Texas A&M's president threatened to resign over the size of Sherrill's contract but had a change of heart.) And, per the article, the highest-paid college football coach at the time Sherrill negotiated his new deal was Oklahoma's Barry Switzer, who was making about $150,000 per year, including benefits.

Naturally it's important to adjust these figures for inflation. Sherrill's $280,000 salary in 1982 is equivalent to $735,000 in 2021. The average university president was making $167,700 in 2021 dollars, and the highest-paid president was making $309,700. This means that, in constant, inflation-adjusted dollars, Swinney's $93 million deal is *more than twenty times larger* than Sherrill's six-year $1.7 million contract, which caused such shock and outrage when it was announced during what was my senior year in college.

Meanwhile, across America's colleges and universities, how many people are being paid more, in real dollars, than the highest-paid university president was being paid in 1982? The answer is many, many thousands. (In 2017, more than 650 college and university presidents were being paid more than this, while 81 received more than $1 million in annual compensation. Furthermore, at almost no major university is the president now the highest-paid employee, who is generally either a football or basketball coach, or the manager of the institution's endowment.)

And the logic of "the market" as it operates in the multibillion-dollar world of big-time college sports has ripple effects throughout the system. For example, Clemson's president was paid $1,016,733 in 2017. This is 228 percent more, in real dollars, than the highest-paid university president in the country was paid when Jackie Sherrill was making his big score, but it nevertheless still represents barely a month of Clemson's football coach's current salary.

As the money frenzy that has overwhelmed college football has driven coaching compensation to levels that would have been literally unimaginable in the simpler, more innocent time when a $280,000 salary was considered shocking, various people have been pointing out that this orgy at the Temple of Mammon is made possible by the striking fact that the players who are responsible for generating billions of dollars per year in revenue have traditionally received no direct compensation, other than the company scrip of "athletic scholarships." Shouldn't they too get a piece of the action, as it were?

No one is more fundamentally offended by this idea than Dabo Swinney. Indeed, the $93 million man has claimed that he'll just walk away from it all if his players start getting paid anything:

> We try to teach our guys, use football to create the opportunities. Take advantage of the brand and the marketing you have available to you.

[Does everyone have to talk like a McKinsey consultant now?] But as far as paying players, professionalizing college athletics, that's where you lose me. *I'll go do something else, because there's enough entitlement in this world as it is.*

That Swinney was not instantly incinerated by thunderbolt after these words left his mouth is another piece of evidence for the view that our particular corner of the cosmos is being managed by an indifferent if not actively malevolent demiurge.

Yet Swinney's perspective on this question, bizarre as it might seem, remains rampant among the powers that be who run big-time college sports. A confidential document from the spring of 2019, recording the views of fifty-two university presidents, athletic directors, and conference commissioners contains reformist insights like this one:

> The biggest threat is that the court system will force us to start paying athletes. And that will be the end of amateur sports as we know it. I think that if we did a better job to show the academic benefits of playing college sports, it would take a lot of wind out of the balloon. *All of the perks like letter jackets, cost of attendance, [team] ring, etc.*

Somehow this reminds me of Orwell's observation that even a writer like Dickens, who hated the very idea of revolution with every fiber of his being, still acknowledged in *A Tale of Two Cities* that, in the end, "the French aristocracy had dug their own graves." I imagine the author of *Democracy in America* would have agreed.

BEING THERE

Twenty years into the new century, the American sports world is confronting a potential problem: people aren't going to the games as much as they used to. The statistics are striking: major league baseball attendance has been on a downward trend for a dozen years now and was 14 percent lower in 2019 than in 2007. That same year, NFL attendance hit a fifteen-year low. The numbers for college football are even more foreboding. Average attendance at major college football games was lower in 2018 than it had been in any year since 1996, even though the nation's population had grown by 22 percent over this time. And these figures might understate the actual decline: a 2018 *Wall Street Journal* report found that nearly 30 percent of the tickets sold to college football games were going unused.

College football's attendance problem is highlighted by the fact that, in 2018, a Clemson team that went undefeated and won the national championship was, even in the heart of the college football–crazed South, unable to sell out even one of its home games. But signs of trouble are everywhere: Ohio State's juggernaut program, which trampled all over the Big Ten conference for the entire decade, saw a 24 percent decline in student ticket sales between 2018 and 2019, even though the Buckeyes were coming off yet another conference championship.

What's going on? The most obvious culprit is the rising cost of attendance, which has affected student attendance in particular, in part because simply attending college is so much more expensive than it used to be. When I was an undergraduate in Ann Arbor in the early 1980s, I (or more accurately, my parents) paid about $4,500 per year *in 2021 dollars* in resident tuition—and Michigan was at the time the most expensive public university in the country. Now Michigan resident undergraduate tuition is nearly four times higher, in real terms. This increase is modest, however, in comparison to the increase in the law school's tuition, which is six times higher, again in real terms, compared to what I paid in the late 1980s.

College football has, understandably, always counted on students to make up a significant percentage of the people in the seats. Predictably, the skyrocketing cost of going to school has combined with massive increases in ticket prices to make the prospect of spending several hours on Saturday participating in a traditional student ritual—realistically, a huge number of the students at college football games are never going to be genuine fans in even a tenuous sense—much less attractive than it used to be.

Another factor that is probably hurting attendance across the board is the startling increase in how long the games last. For example, throughout the 1970s the average major league baseball game lasted two and a half hours: the same figure for 2021 was three hours and ten minutes. But this increase is modest in comparison to what has happened in college football. In 1973, as a thirteen-year-old boy, I went to every Michigan home game: those games averaged two hours and twenty-eight minutes. This past season, the *shortest* Michigan game was nearly a full hour longer, and games approaching four hours are now far from unusual.

A minor, though still annoying, factor driving this increase has been the ridiculous replay system employed by college football, which leads to often-pointless delays to review officiating decisions that wouldn't be reviewed in a more rational system, such as that used in the NFL. College football can't copy the NFL, however, as doing so might imply that this multibillion-dollar enterprise isn't a purely amateur endeavor.

But by far the most important factor in the lengthening of games has been the requirements of television, which provides an increasingly large share of the money that makes the whole thing go. It's a striking fact that, back in 1973, games were broadcast in such a way that televised games—which were rare at the time—didn't last any longer than those that weren't televised. The titanic clash that year between the undefeated and top-ranked Michigan and Ohio State teams was televised nationally, but ended up being three minutes shorter than the average Michigan game that season.

In the early 1970s, a national college football broadcast would, as a matter of contractual obligation, include a total of eighteen minutes of commercials (including during halftime). Natural breaks in the action, such as those after scoring plays, between quarters, and to tend to injured players, happened often enough that it was possible to televise a game without lengthening the time it took to play it, as amazing as that proposition may seem to fans today, especially those in the stands, who must endure interminable "TV time outs" in order to feed the multibillion-dollar beast that college football has become. Today, the typical college football broadcast will include nearly a full hour of official commercial breaks—but the actual time spent on commercial interruptions is significantly longer, since this figure doesn't include things like in-game promos and banner ads.

It's hardly a surprise that younger fans, who have grown up in an Internet-saturated world in which attention spans are being constantly decreased by the economic imperatives of a clickbait culture, are increasingly resisting the idea of sitting in a possibly broiling or freezing stadium for nearly four hours. This is all the more likely to be the case given that fans there often having little or no access to the online world that is their natural milieu: Internet connectivity is a perpetual problem at events where tens of thousands of people are gathered in a small space. Such factors make it more difficult to convince young fans in general, and college students in particular, that attending the Big Game in person represents a desirable investment of their scarce discretionary income.

Up until now, the declining attendance at most big-time sports events in America (the NBA is a notable exception) has elicited relatively mild concern from the powers that be, for a straightforward reason: the overall revenues these sports generate continue to grow. All these enterprises are becoming ever more dependent on television money, and other licensing arrangements—Internet streaming, merchandise sales, etc.—rather than ticket sales.

Despite declining attendance, total revenues for major league baseball nearly doubled between 2007 and 2019, from $5.5 billion to more than $10 billion per year. During the same time, NFL annual revenue more than doubled, from $7 billion to $15 billion; the league remains on track to hit its target of generating $25 billion per year by 2027. Changes in total college football revenue are harder to calculate accurately; still, consider that Michigan's athletic department is now annually bringing in three times as much money, in inflation-adjusted terms, as it was just twenty years ago.

Nevertheless, it's difficult to imagine that, even in the brave new world of multibillion-dollar media rights and licensing packages, revenue and attendance can continue to move in opposite directions for too much longer. The fundamental problem was described nearly thirty years ago by Nick Hornby—although the fact that he did so almost three decades ago should give pause to anyone who is prone to make overconfident predictions about how much longer anything in the world of sports can actually go on.

Hornby described how, in England in the 1980s, the televising of soccer moved almost overnight from an arrangement in which only a tiny number of games were ever on TV to one in which the clubs became willing to do anything and everything to put their games on the screen. A very similar thing happened, at roughly the same time, in college football. "Eventually," Hornby wrote, "the clubs realized there was big money to be made, and the TV companies were happy to give it to them."

With enormous sums being dangled before it, the league suddenly became solicitous of every whim of the television industry: the starting times, and even the days on which games were played, were liable to change at any moment, to the point where the information printed on one's ticket became largely meaningless. "Meanwhile, the fans," Hornby remarks, "the paying customers, are regarded as amenable and gullible idiots." He gives an example of a crucial out-of-town game for Arsenal—a London club—in which, to accommodate television, the starting time was changed so that the game would end after the last train back to London had already left. "Who cared? Just us, nobody important." Hornby predicted,

> Television will notice our absence, one day. In the end, no matter how much they mike up the crowd, they will be unable to create any atmosphere whatsoever, because there will be nobody there; we'll all be at home, watching the box. And when that happens, I hope the managers and the chairmen spare us the pompous and embittered column in the programme complaining about our fickleness.

At its heart, the problem is that in-person attendance often plays a crucial role in creating the kind of lifelong deep engagement on which all these immensely profitable enterprises depend. Those visceral childhood memories of the first time you emerged out of the darkness of the tunnel and saw that vast expanse of green, that enormous crowd—that whole mysterious, essentially adult world to which you were now beginning to gain entrance—cannot be replaced by even the most comprehensive cable or Internet package.

And beyond this, sitting and standing, cheering and cursing with your fellow fans, while, like Lear on the heath, enduring all of nature's fury rather than curling up comfortably in front of a gigantic high-definition television set, is the kind of counterintuitive, essentially anti-utilitarian gesture of communal loyalty and dedication that makes a deeply engaged fan something more than just another fickle consumer, and spectator sports something more, at least occasionally, than just another form of casual entertainment.

Will the coming generations of fans, with mobile devices that give us all access to the entire world of entertainment, sporting and otherwise, at essentially all times and places, continue to indulge, as we older fans have, the rapacious hunger for ever more revenue that has made actually being there such an expensive and burdensome experience? The COVID-19 pandemic is producing something of a natural experiment along these lines, as much of the sporting world was deprived of all or nearly all spectators in 2020. The almost universal return of large crowds in 2021 suggests that, at least for now, the desire of fans to actually be there in person remains fairly strong, despite all the factors pushing them to stay home.

It goes without saying that the lords of capital will continue to treat deeply engaged fans as the endlessly exploitable marks that— let's face it—our addiction more or less ensures we will remain. But no one is required or fated to become deeply engaged fan in the first place. This particular golden goose, like any other, isn't immortal; and those who continue to gather ever more staggering profits from it would do well to remember that fact.

CELEBRATION DAY

One of the many charms of the old video clips of sports events now so easily accessible on the Internet is that they allow us to trace the historical evolution of social rituals such as those expected to accompany victory celebrations. Specifically, the contrast between how athletes today and those in the not-so-distant past acknowledged the greatest moments of their athletic careers is striking.

Compare, for example, Rod Laver's reaction to winning Wimbledon in 1968 to how Rafael Nadal reacted to winning the 2019 US Open. I chose these examples more or less at random: any comparison of the celebration of major tennis championship victories between these eras would reveal much the same. On match point, Laver hits a clean winner; he then simply comes to the net and shakes his opponent Tony Roche's hand, before giving him a quick pat on the back. His only evident display of emotion consists of flipping the tennis ball in his hand up in the air, in what seems, from today's perspective, a very muted gesture of elation by someone who has just won the most important title in his sport.

Nadal, by contrast, sees Dani Medvedev's return of his serve sail long and instantly collapses onto the court. He assumes a spread-eagle posture, which the director of the telecast shows us from directly above. The Spaniard has an expression of agonistic triumph; for a moment the tableau looks like an El Greco portrait of some sort of ecstatic martyrdom: *The Passion of the Center Court*. He finally pulls himself to his feet and slowly jogs to the net, where he embraces Medvedev warmly, puts his arm around his young opponent's shoulder, and utters what we can assume are words of gracious consolation in his ear.

It's not just tennis. Compare the respective last outs of the decisive seventh games of the 1965 and 2019 World Series. In 1965, Sandy Koufax, starting for the third time in just eight days, wraps up perhaps the most famous performance of his storied career, clinching the championship for his team by striking out Minnesota's Bob Allison to complete an epic three-hit shutout. After Allison swings and misses, Koufax does nothing but smile and walk toward catcher John Roseboro, who simply shakes his hand. Several teammates surround him and pat him on the shoulder as they all jog into the dugout. Everyone seems quite pleased, but by today's standards it resembles a restrained celebration of an ordinary win on a sleepy mid-season afternoon, as opposed to a victory in the biggest of all possible baseball games.

In 2019, Washington Nationals relief pitcher Daniel Hudson strikes out Houston Astros outfielder Michael Brantley to complete his team's 6–2 win in the series' decisive game. Hudson leaps into the air, hurls his glove toward the dugout, and is almost immediately mobbed by all his teammates, who rush the mound and then jump up and down with their arms around each other in the middle of the infield for nearly a full minute.

In all the high-profile sports, players' informal celebrations of important victories are strikingly more demonstrative and effusive than they were a few decades ago. Meanwhile, the formal recognition of those triumphs has undergone an even more striking transformation. While previously the postgame celebration generally took place in the locker room, to which players retreated as soon as the game ended, today it takes place out on the field or the court. With lightning speed, a temporary stage is assembled, confetti and balloons descend from the skies, strobe lights flash, triumphal music blares, and a parade of speakers is brought onto that stage, during which the team's ownership, coaches, and players will express how thrilled they are to the fans in attendance and the vastly larger audience watching on TV. Generally, these speeches are as stylized as the liturgy of a Catholic mass. Speakers invariably praise the never-surrender spirit of everyone on the entire team—a team that overcame remarkable adversity and that no one believed in at the beginning of the season. (This latter claim will sometimes but not always be tastefully omitted in the case of a team that has won several championships recently.)

Even though contemporary fans have now seen this ceremony and heard these speeches countless times, we would no doubt feel cheated if it weren't provided. Indeed, if the celebration at the end of the seventh game of the World Series were to suddenly revert to the style prevalent in 1965, we would probably react like viewers of a romantic comedy that concluded with a murder-suicide, or a *Star Wars* movie that ended with the Death Star still intact.

All these changes reflect more general trends in the world of entertainment, and sports in particular. Sociologically speaking, the word "hypertrophy" refers to elaboration of some cultural practice beyond any immediately apparent practical need or function. The Egyptian pyramids are a classic example: what began as a simple ceremony to help the soul's journey to the afterworld—placing a cup and a dish in the grave of the deceased, for instance—eventually became something that required dedicating a large portion of the kingdom's economic activity to the building of monumental tombs.

In the contemporary sports world, we are subjected constantly to, as it were, the hypertrophy of hype. As the economics of big-time sports grow ever more extreme, everyone involved is under pressure, whether conscious or unconscious, to play up the supposed significance of what fans are paying so much to witness. For example, when Sandy Koufax was pitching that seventh-game shutout, the average major league salary was about $18,000 per year—$156,000 in 2021 dollars. This past season, the average was $4.43 million: a nearly thirty-fold increase in real, inflation-adjusted dollars. Yet both the value and the profitability of the franchises that were paying out these stupendous salaries were at all-time highs.

Baseball is in no way unusual in this regard: Rod Laver was awarded the princely sum of $2,621 for winning the 1968 Wimbledon men's title, while Rafael Nadal received $3.85 million for his US Open win in 2019.

In a world of money madness and media saturation, in which competition for the ever-expanding entertainment dollar becomes ever more ferocious, fans are bombarded at every minute of every day by increasingly strident demands that they pay attention to this or that Big Event, which is treated by the entertainment industrial complex as the most important and exciting thing of its kind that has ever happened—at least until next season, or next week, or later that night. Under such conditions, it's hardly surprising that players end up playing along, consciously or unconsciously, with a media hype machine that tries to turn a Monday night football game into a clash of world-historical significance, as opposed to something that will determine first place in the NFC West, at least for the moment.

There is, after all, nothing natural about the idea that a baseball or football game is some sort of big deal. Players need to be accultur-ated to the supposed significance of what they're doing every bit as much as do the fans who are paying to watch them. And the more we fans pay for that privilege, the more excited players become, or seem to become, about the contests that are yielding them such im-mense incomes.

I am not saying that contemporary athletes' florid representations of the thrill of victory and the agony of defeat are insincere. Athletes no doubt sincerely react, for the most part, to thrilling victories and agonizing defeats, because they, like their fans, have learned from the earliest age that sports genuinely matter. The enormous paychecks the most successful professional athletes now receive surely make that belief more concrete as a practical matter, both to them and to us. This is what economists call "revealed preference"—if you want to know what people really care about, as opposed to what they say they care about, look at how they spend their money.

That essentially plutocratic principle is not exactly ennobling, given what we as a society actually choose to spend our money on, but it does have the advantage of throwing our often-indefensible preferences and practices into stark relief. In contemporary America, what we celebrate more than anything else are money, fame, and the successful pursuit of both. Athletes' increasingly elaborate celebra-tions of their own successes are, once again, a demonstration of how sports and the rituals that surround them are ultimately reflections of their larger society.

OK BOOMER

Everyone born toward the tail end or in the wake of the baby boom is acutely aware of how we've spent our whole lives in a culture dominated by the cultural and political obsessions of our elders. In 2021, the Rolling Stones were on tour, while men and women who are even older than Mick Jagger dominated the American political landscape.

In the world of sports, a striking reminder of this culture-wide gerontocracy is the persistence of so many of the same TV personalities who have been broadcasting games since the 1970s, if not earlier. Brent Musburger, Dick Stockton, Marv Albert, Al Michaels, Dick Vitale, Verne Lundquist, Bob Costas . . . so many of these guys—not coincidentally, they are all white guys—have been around seemingly forever. Imagine if in 1975 sports broadcasting had been full of people who had been on the national airways since the Hoover administration.

Thus does the ubiquity of the baby boom and the imperatives of advertising combine to ensure that middle-aged sports fans will still hear the comfortably familiar intonations of so many of the same voices we were listening to when we were teenagers, just as surely as we can count on hearing, for approximately the 2,500th time, the melancholy country rock musings of James Taylor circa 1975, even if we're just shopping for avocados at Safeway.

One consequence of this situation is that sports broadcasting is full of—at least in terms of sports knowledge—reactionaries, who continue to relay the conventional wisdom of their youth to an audience that is increasingly aware that much of that supposed wisdom is non-sense. For instance, it's striking how, in the context of the scoring fest that is college football today, boomer announcers are still living in a world in which the final score of the Big Game was likely to be something like 17–10. To these people, field position is the most precious thing in the world, and the most important thing an offense can do is pick up a first down or two, so that when the team punts the other team will have to go the length of the field to score, which these announcers continue to consider a rare feat, despite what's happening now before their very eyes.

Example: In November of 2019 I watch Alabama and Auburn provide a particularly thrilling version of their classic annual rivalry. Alabama scores yet again to go up 30–24 with a minute left in the first half; Auburn then takes over after the kick return at their own 35. Boomer announcer Gary Danielson predictably intones the conventional wisdom of his youth: Auburn really needs to be careful here, as they have a freshman quarterback, and a turnover could be extremely costly. Better to just call a couple of conservative handoffs and get to the locker room still down by only one score.

Danielson doesn't seem to notice that Alabama is scoring on almost every possession. They've got wall-to-wall five-star recruits and a defensive guru of a head coach. The Crimson Tide also have a kid named Jaylen Waddle, who accelerates to approximately 12 percent of the speed of light in about two steps, and as a consequence seems to score a touchdown every third time he touches the ball. Under the circumstances, Auburn has to make the most of every possession. Choosing to waste one because you're afraid something bad might happen overlooks that, in today's college football, not scoring any time you have the ball *is* something bad happening.

But we hear things like this over and over again, especially but far from exclusively from the voices of experienced wisdom. What this sort of analysis represents is, above all, overwhelming loss aversion, in which the advice is always to avoid the most immediate potential bad outcome, at the cost of exacerbating the risk of much worse outcomes just a little further along down the decisional road. As we've seen, people in general, and sports fans in particular, tend to be loss averse, even when loss aversion is, strategically speaking, seriously suboptimal. But part of this is also clearly generational.

Fortunately, despite its remarkable resilience, this sort of reactionary thinking has been under increasingly successful attack for a generation now. I well remember a morning in March of 1984 when, in a Hyde Park bookstore on the South Side of Chicago, I came across a book with the oddly scholastic title of *The Baseball Abstract*. The author's name was vaguely familiar: I remembered having read something in *Sports Illustrated* about how Bill James was bringing a new analytical approach to the game, in which he used a home computer— still a rare and exotic device at that time—to break down traditional statistics into new and more valuable forms. Over the next few years, I was thrilled to see that what James dubbed "sabermetrics"—the use of statistical analysis to critique conventional baseball wisdom— would begin to affect not only how the game was talked about by fans and journalists but how it was played. Forward-thinking executives such as the Oakland A's general manager Billy Beane used sabermetric knowledge to gain an upper hand over Goliath organizations featuring much bigger payrolls that were nevertheless hampered by their worship of an increasingly bankrupt conventional wisdom.

And the statistical revolution did not stop there: soon, the empirical and contrarian impulses behind sabermetrics spread to other sports, as people running football, basketball, soccer, and other big-money enterprises looked for their own analytic edges in an increasingly hypercompetitive world. Suddenly it seemed possible to be a sports fan without also being an intellectually reactionary follower of mindless traditionalism.

In that vein, one topic I spent years obsessing about on the message board was punting—that is, voluntarily kicking the ball to the other team on fourth down, rather than trying to maintain possession by gaining the necessary yardage. "A punt is a turnover!" I would fulminate to my fellow obsessives. Conventional football wisdom continues to hold that turning the ball over via a fumble or an interception is an absolute disaster, to be avoided at almost all costs. Mysteriously enough, turning the ball over by punting it to the other team has always been treated as a completely different thing.

Of course I remember the precise moment when my frustration on this topic reached a boiling point: October 30, 1999. Michigan was playing Indiana in Bloomington, and the Wolverines featured an offense made up almost entirely of future NFL players, including eventual superstars such as quarterback Tom Brady and offensive lineman Chris Hutchinson. Meanwhile, Indiana's quarterback Antwaan Randle El—also a future NFL star—was that afternoon a kind of offensive wizard, whom Michigan's defense strove to contain with little success. Tied late in the third quarter, Michigan was faced with fourth down and 1 yard to go on the Indiana 41-yard line. To my amazement (this is a rhetorical phrase—I was completely unsurprised), Michigan's coach, the classically conservative Lloyd Carr, decided to punt. Predictably, the punt went into the end zone, which gave Indiana the ball at their own 20—a net change in field position of 21 yards. Even more predictably, on the first play after the change of possession Randle El proceeded to gain back 19 of those precious 21 yards by eluding a host of befuddled Michigan defenders. So Michigan had given up the ball, forgoing an excellent chance of maintaining possession by converting on fourth down, just so Indiana could end up having the ball at almost exactly the same spot, one play later.

In so-called real life, I wanted to scream in frustration. Luckily, the board, open on my laptop in front of the TV, allowed me to scream for the two hundredth time to my fellow sufferers that a punt is a turnover.

Thus I considered it an almost personal vindication when, a few years later, University of California economist David Romer demonstrated with mathematical rigor that coaches did punt far too often, given the relevant probabilities. Romer's paper—which is technically about the more academically respectable topic of the extent to which firms maximize profit-making opportunities—showed that the conventional wisdom about punting was radically wrong. His conclusions suggest that coaches punt far too often because they frame losing the ball on downs as a bad thing, while interpreting giving the ball away via a punt as, if not exactly a good thing, then not nearly as bad an event. And of course it isn't nearly as bad—*if you ignore the opportunity cost of forgoing the chance of keeping the ball*. But that opportunity cost is, Romer demonstrated, massive: so much so that coaches should go for a first down in situations where, according to the conventional wisdom, doing so would be considered the height of recklessness.

As big-money sports become ever more profitable and competitive, the cost of ignoring the insights of people like James and Romer becomes ever greater. Indeed, shortly after Romer's paper appeared, it found an apparently unlikely reader: New England Patriots' coach Bill Belichick. Belichick adopted much of Romer's analysis to his own in-game decision-making, with predictably successful results. (In 2004, I authored, along with my friend and fellow Michigan fanatic Jon Chait, a piece for the *New York Times* in which we discussed Belichick's use of Romer's work.)

So change does come, if slowly: there are still plenty of coaches who make indefensible tactical decisions during games, not only in regard to punting but in terms of other easily quantifiable statistical decisions, such as clock management and two-point conversion attempts. (Such miscalculations remain a favorite board topic, especially during the hysteria of in-game posting.) Still, teams in many sports are, as a matter of rational self-interest, increasingly abetting a kind of revenge of the nerds, in which analytic types find themselves in the front office and even on the sidelines, as they advise teams on how to acquire talent in the most efficient way, and how to deploy it most effectively on game day.

This revolution, like all revolutions, remains controversial. For no-doubt complicated sociological reasons, team sports seem to draw more than their share of reactionaries in a broader sense. So we have the sorry spectacle of longtime high-profile sportswriters such as Murray Chass and Dan Shaughnessy, who, in the words of *Deadspin*, "never tire of ridiculing sabermetricians as limp-wristed geeks living in their mothers' basements," thus illustrating how a certain aggressively stupid traditional masculinity continues to be the hallmark of so much sports journalism.

Fortunately, as the relentless march of demographics ensures that the boomer generation fades from the scene, today's reactionaries in the world of sports will suffer the same fate that awaits the median

Fox News viewer, who at present is a sixty-five-year-old white man. Whether that development manages to arrest America's current slide toward authoritarian ethno-nationalism remains to be seen. But we can at least hope that it will continue to make fans of all sports less tolerant of a conventional wisdom that is too often either banal or idiotic or both. If the intolerance of youth for the stupidity of age can't save liberal democracy, perhaps it can at least eventually produce more tolerable sports broadcasting.

A FLAG IS DOWN

American football is a particularly stupid and indefensible sport. The stupidity of the whole enterprise was driven home to me some years ago when I was deputized by my employer to entertain an eminent foreigner, who for some reason wished to attend an NFL game. In the course of attempting to carry out my responsibilities, I tried to explain various aspects of the rules of the sport to my visitor, who knew essentially nothing about it.

I soon realized that, despite having seen literally thousands of football games over several decades, I could not explain the rules of the game to someone who wasn't already familiar with it. Why, to pick one of an almost unlimited number of examples, must the offense have exactly seven players on the line of scrimmage? Whatever the original practical justification, if any, this rule has been obviated by the fact that the "line of scrimmage" can be avoided by any player who is a half step behind the ball. Yet in a huge percentage of games a penalty will end up being called because a slot receiver wasn't a half step back from the line, or because some similar completely nonsensical rule has been violated inadvertently.

This mindless obeisance to pointlessly complicated formal rules is combined with a wildly arbitrary enforcement mechanism. My many thousands of hours of football viewing didn't allow me to explain to my guest what "pass interference" consists of, since the enforcement of that critical rule varies so radically between officials, even at the NFL level, that any description requires a level of abstraction that makes that description useless. A similar point can be made about what constitutes "holding" by an offensive lineman, which could be called on literally every play if the rules as written were enforced in a comprehensive and consistent way.

It's true that all rule regimes, in life as well as sports, feature gray areas; but, in American football, it sometimes seems that many of the most important rules are almost nothing but gray area. This circumstance produces a level of necessarily arbitrary enforcement that allows all fans at all times to believe, and with some justice, that their team is being robbed by the officiating powers that be.

Add to this the basic impossibility of a seven-person officiating crew applying those rules in a consistent way to a sport involving a dozen or more frighteningly enormous and unbelievably fast men crashing into one another in a series of extremely rapid and fantastically violent collisions, all within a relatively tiny space where it's difficult to see exactly what's happening with the help of slow-motion replay, let alone at actual game speed with the unaided human eye.

And, leaving aside all this, many of the formal rules are interpreted within a kind of common law system of official discretion that ignores the rules as written in ways that must be incomprehensible to anyone not already familiar with the baroque complexity of these interpretive practices. For example, I had to explain to my guest why the quarterback throwing the ball thirty feet over everyone's head into the tenth row of the end zone seats to avoid a sack isn't intentional grounding, even though the rules state that the penalty applies to throwing the ball to an area without a receiver in order to avoid a sack. The answer is, because that's just the way the rule is called by officials, usually.

Again, it's true that most rule systems feature informal deviations, along with gray areas, less than optimal official knowledge, and other epistemological quandaries. But what's particularly striking about American football is how extreme these phenomena are, relative to other sports. Consider the sport that the rest of the world calls football, a.k.a. soccer: The rules are extremely simple, intuitive, and liable to much less interpretive arbitrariness and official discretion—although of course there is still a good deal of this at the margins. But the simplicity of the rules ensures that there are far fewer margins.

In addition, American football seems obsessed with enforcing a kind of parody of bureaucratic rationality that flies directly in the face of the actual structure of the game. Imagine trying to explain to a novice the process by which it's determined that a ball carrier has or has not advanced far enough to achieve a first down. This decision is supposed to be made with precision, within a margin of considerably less than an inch. That is of course completely absurd: the placement of the ball after a tackle is often essentially arbitrary within tolerances of at least a foot, given the difficulty of determining exactly when and where a ball carrier's forward progress was arrested as he flew into a chaotic mass of humanity.

This kind of ridiculous hyper-bureaucratization has only been exacerbated by the introduction of replay review, which now allows for long delays, during which a half dozen officials hold abstruse discussions of exactly how the rules of the game ought to be applied, in situations where the rules themselves are often unclear or contradictory and the empirical precision necessary to employ them properly—where exactly the ball should be spotted, for example—is wholly absent.

In short, it's difficult to imagine people who haven't been acculturated from a young age to the idea that both the rules of American football and their application make some sort of minimal sense coming independently to the conclusion that they do. This is probably the biggest reason why American football, in stark contrast to both baseball and basketball, has had so little success in establishing itself in other cultures.

But ultimately the absurdity of football's rules, and the arbitrariness of their application, are merely aesthetic quibbles. From an ethical perspective, a much more problematic aspect is how the physics of the game make it difficult to play without doing permanent long-term physical damage, and especially cognitive damage, to so many of its players. Those physics are reflected in Newton's basic equations of motion, which state, more or less, that if a large fast-moving object collides with another such object in such a way that both deaccelerate almost instantly, then the resulting maximum force of that collision is going to be hazardous to the short- and long-term health of those objects, if they happen to be human beings.

And this hazard has become increasingly worse. When I was first entranced by Michigan football back in the 1970s, the players were both a little slower and a great deal smaller than they are today. In 1976, Michigan's defensive line averaged 219 pounds. In 2020, Michigan's defensive line averaged 285 pounds—and the lack of "big" defensive tackles was considered a team weakness. Meanwhile in the NFL, offensive linemen now average 315 pounds: 60 pounds more than in the 1970s.

A combination of much more rigorous training methods and increasingly sophisticated pharmaceutical interventions have created a generation of players who make their recent predecessors look almost like children by comparison and who perform physical feats on the field that are difficult to comprehend. For instance, during the 2020 playoff game between the Philadelphia Eagles and Seattle Seahawks, Philadelphia's defensive tackle Fletcher Cox repeatedly tossed Seattle's center around as if he were a rag doll rather than a superbly conditioned 300-pound professional athlete.

The result is that pretty much every play in a big-time college football game—let alone in the NFL—features the equivalent of several car crashes. The combination of high-definition television and an age-related increasing awareness of the fragility of the human body often leave me wondering how every play doesn't result in several serious injuries.

It isn't as if the football of the 1970s wasn't extremely violent: I still, for example, remember vividly the bull-like running back Earl Campbell planting his helmet between the five and the eight on the front of star Los Angeles linebacker Isiah Robertson's jersey, sending him flying 5 yards backward. I also recall Campbell himself getting obviously concussed at the goal line from an incredibly vicious hit delivered by the infamous Oakland Raiders' headhunter Jack Tatum, while somehow still toppling forward into the end zone.

The risk of concussion inherent to the game explains the astonishing prevalence of chronic traumatic encephalopathy (CTE) among NFL players. A 2017 study published in the *Journal of the American Medical Association* found evidence of the disease—which can be diagnosed definitively only after death—in 110 of 111 players.

The effects of this disease are devastating. In 2018, Emily Kelly, the wife of former NFL player Rob Kelly, drew a horrifying portrait of what football had done to her husband. Once a gentle and attentive spouse and father, Rob Kelly had become almost unrecognizable:

> Our fights went in bizarre circles and were never resolved. He would be irrationally upset about one thing but would quickly lose track and begin rambling about something that had no connection to the topic at hand. Every argument we had ended with me thinking: "This isn't normal. This is not what couples fight about. Something's wrong." . . .
>
> He was losing touch with reality and was getting more and more paranoid. The first time he accused me of stealing loose change from his nightstand I was speechless. And when I told him how illogical it would be for me to do such a thing, he looked at me with even more suspicion. But his paranoia didn't end there. It would leave me with a heaviness in my chest that made me sob without warning.

Emily Kelly discovered that the nightmarish transformation that had robbed her of the man she married was far from unusual among NFL players. She found a private Facebook group of more than 2,400 women, all connected to current or former NFL players. The stories she heard were terribly familiar: sudden mood swings, inexplicable outbursts of rage, obsessive behavior, chronic depression, increasingly severe memory loss.

Reading Kelly's article, or the similarly heartrending account from Tracy Lytle, widow of Rob Lytle, hero of that 1976 Michigan–Ohio State game, or delving into the growing medical literature on what high-level football actually does to the boys and men who play it, ought to give serious pause to anyone who continues to patronize the game. Can football in anything like its present form continue to flourish? The NFL's much-advertised rule changes, intended to address the concussion crisis, ignore the evidence suggesting that CTE and related cognitive maladies are more a product of hundreds or thousands of microconcussions over the years than of the especially gruesome collisions these changes are meant to ameliorate.

As the evidence of the devastating effects of the sport mounts, it will become increasingly common for middle- and upper-class parents to flatly refuse to subject their children to it. As this happens, the sport will, like boxing before it, become a kind of gladiatorial contest, engaged in by the sons of the desperate and the indifferent.

As with so many other issues in America today, football is becoming a flashpoint in the culture wars, as progressives in particular come to terms with subsidizing a sport that they would under no circumstances allow their own children to play. And, again characteristically, our most recent ex-president has thrown this particular battle into sharp and crude relief: At a campaign rally in Alabama in 2017, Donald Trump complained that rule changes are "ruining the game." "Today, if you hit too hard, 15 yards, throw him out of the game!" Trump fumed, as he whipped this crowd, in the very heart of football country, into a frenzy over the ongoing sissification of a once-great nation by latte-sipping social justice warriors.

One possible result of this war will be the increasing salience, in both economic and political terms, of the other football in twenty-first-century America. Soccer—which has its own, though considerably less severe, problem with concussions—is gaining traction, especially among young people, as an alternative to football, which more and more is becoming associated with the culture and politics of Trumplandia.

Indeed, the NFL's embrace of aggressively militaristic nationalism—every other week of the season seems to feature another salute to Our Heroes Who Keep Us Safe—and its disgraceful handling of African American quarterback Colin Kaepernick's symbolic kneeling on the sideline in protest against police violence both serve as reminders that, culturally speaking, football has always been a fundamentally reactionary sport. A similar reminder was provided by the NCAA's long-standing enthusiasm for making sure that football and basketball players, who are overwhelmingly African American, worked as quasi-indentured servants, for the enrichment of an ever more sanctimonious and hypocritical caste of mostly old white guys. Recent legal decisions empowering players seem to be quelling that enthusiasm, at least.

On one level, it would of course be far more pleasant to keep politics out of sports. But there is no keeping out of politics in an age like this—which, in that respect, is very much like all the ages before it. Ultimately, as American culture and politics become ever darker and more divisive, the time may come when people who oppose reactionary politics may find it necessary to reject definitively a sport they have loved. Or perhaps that time is already here, and people like me simply refuse to look that particular truth, like so many other uncomfortable truths, in the face.

BACON AND THE PATRIARCHY

By a simple yet cruel twist of fate, I just missed witnessing the greatest upset victory in the 140-year history of Michigan football. When Michigan defeated the legendary 1969 Ohio State Buckeyes—a team that some sportswriters held could only be defeated by an NFL squad rather than by any college opponent—I was all of 5.2 miles away. Still, the game might as well have been played in the Andromeda galaxy, as at that moment I was unaware something called Michigan football even existed. Soon enough I would be putting the fan in fanatical, but that afternoon I was doing something else altogether, to the subsequent amazement of my subsequent self.

So it is that today, decades later, I must content myself with watching the complete ABC broadcast of the first half of the game, uploaded to YouTube by one Chuck Phillips (may his name be praised). In addition to the game action, this upload includes a delightful trove of cultural studies arcana: the commercials. One commercial in particular—for Wilson Certified Bacon—offers a not-so-distant window onto the past. Its almost completely stationary single camera focuses on the pitchman, Paul Christman. Christman had been a minor NFL star twenty years earlier and went on to become a broadcaster. (At the very time he was recording this commercial, his teenage daughter ran off to Haight-Asbury and got mixed up with Scientology, which she eventually broke away from, becoming one of its most prominent public critics, which she remains to this day. The engaged fan can find rabbit holes everywhere.)

While delivering his spiel, Christman doesn't do anything except hold up a package of Wilson Certified Bacon while standing in a faux kitchen, though he does sit down at a puritanically furnished table midpitch. Besides lacking any kinetic energy, the commercial features no music—indeed, compared to the attention deficit disorder frenzy that characterizes television advertising fifty years later, it's amazing how little happens during the spot. This was a national television broadcast, so this ad was no doubt produced by the Mad Men of the time. (One Don Draperesque touch is that at no point are we informed what "certified" means, even though the word is repeated several times.)

Most striking of all, there's no appearance of the ambrosial substance that, according to Christman's domestic gospel, will save the family breakfast. This is simply perverse: surely the beauty of bacon, from an advertorial point of view, is that it *looks* so good sizzling in its own fat. Christman even tells us that it's the kind of bacon that "looks good in the pan." But where's the star of the show?

The real interpretive crux of this text is provided in the last fifteen seconds. After lauding the infinite variety of Wilson Certified Bacon—other bacons cloy the appetites they feed, while Wilson's makes hungry where most it satisfies—Christman looks straight into the camera and says: "Why not tell your wife to try some tomorrow? And, if she comes home with a different brand, send her back for Wilson's Certified. Just remember this: it's the marvelous meat that makes the big difference."

Initially, this passage seemed to me to present something of a hermeneutic puzzle. Was Christman being serious? Or was this kidding on the square, with the putative humor lending a sort of cover of deniability? I've shown the ad to several women who either lived in that era or grew up in families with men who did, and every one of them assured me that Christman was being completely matter of fact, rather than joking, and that my suspicion that I detected a twinkle in his eye was an anachronistic overinterpretation. Apparently, what we are being presented with here is simply the patriarchy in full, unapologetic bloom, despite—or because of—the fact that at this same time second-wave feminists were burning bras and not shaving their legs and getting offended when a traditionally minded gentleman opened a door for them, instead of frying up some bacon for break-fast, as God intended, goddamn it. Of course as the Men's Rights Movement illustrates, "Why is my bitch so disrespectful?" remains a question that so many men, fifty years later, are still asking, even in these politically correct times, when you can't even talk to other men in a manly way anymore, because someone might #MeToo you.

Also, note the apparent assumption that pretty much the entire audience for this telecast consists of married men, who could no more imagine doing something like going to the supermarket to buy their own bacon than they could imagine that Paul Christman might not even like girls or that a woman could be president of the United States someday.

So progress does happen, as difficult as that can sometimes be to remember in this age of reaction and retrenchment.

UPON FURTHER REVIEW, EVERY MAN KILLS THE THING HE LOVES

Over the past two decades, nothing has altered the emotional experience of the deeply engaged fan more than the introduction of replay review. Prior to then, if something happened on the field, then it had happened. And as a fan, you had to deal with it at the moment, because, like the past itself, it could no longer be altered. Replay review has changed all that. Now something has not really happened until the authorities have had a chance to consult technology, to determine if what they initially declared to be the case is in fact the way things are going to be.

Replay review was a probably inevitable consequence of the relentless march of technology. As television cameras and high-definition broadcasting became ubiquitous, every marginal call could be viewed by fans from multiple angles, in slow motion. Predictably, this had the same effect on the tolerance for official error that DNA testing has had on tolerance for claims that wrongful convictions are all but impossible. (In the pre-DNA era, a.k.a. the early 1990s, I heard the district attorney for the city of Denver declare that his office had never secured a wrongful guilty verdict. Claims of this type were actually common at the time.) Thus it came to pass that the NFL adopted a replay review system in 1999, while college football and other big-money team sports followed suit over the course of the following decade.

Bringing more of what Max Weber called the iron cage of bureaucratic rationality into the world of sports has of course had some clear benefits. The main virtue of replay review is the one everyone anticipated when it was adopted: it is certainly true that some egregiously blown calls are now rectified upon further review. But of course there are also significant costs. The most obvious of these are delays in games that, because of the imperatives of television advertising, have already been stretched out to lengths that test the patience of even the most dedicated fans. Another unavoidable cost is how replay review creates an enormous gray zone of bad but ultimately irreversible calls.

The former effect is especially annoying at college games, where, because of the characteristic squeamishness of college officials to merely copy the system used in more openly professional football, every play is subject to replay review, leading to delays to review calls that are either not really close, or trivial, or both. The latter outcome is something that any lawyer could have told you was inevitable: if the standard for reversing a call is, in the words of the official NFL rules, "indisputable visual evidence" that the initial call was wrong, this creates a massive practical gap between calls that are, on the one hand, more likely wrong than not, and on the other, clearly wrong, with the meaning of "clearly" being, inevitably, far from clear. (To assert that evidence is indisputable is merely to beg the question of what "indisputable" means.)

The result is that replay review doesn't eliminate bad calls, even when a call is reviewable—many are not—but instead shifts the question to whether a call is bad enough to reverse. This new controversy is exacerbated by the fact that different officials—also inevitably—end up employing different standards for what constitutes clear error, with some officials seemingly approaching the question as if they had been making the call in the first place, while others treat the original call as presumptively correct, needing overwhelming evidence to reverse. In hyperlegalistic America, the parallels with the different standards applied by different judges in courts of law are striking. And in football in particular, the distinction between reviewable and nonreviewable calls is often as arbitrary as so many other aspects of this most pointlessly complex of games.

For example, in the 2019 NFC championship game between New Orleans and Los Angeles, the referees failed to call an especially egregious instance of pass interference in the final moments of regulation time. Because pass interference is considered a "judgment call" under the replay rules, the (non)call was not reviewable. The failure to call the penalty almost certainly cost New Orleans the game and a subsequent trip to the Super Bowl. Saints fans were understandably outraged. Two of them, Tommy Badeaux and Candis Lambert, went so far as to file a lawsuit against the NFL and its commissioner, Roger Goodell, "individually and on behalf of New Orleans Saints Season Ticket Holders, New Orleans Saints National Fan base a/k/a The Who Dat Nation, and any party with interest that has been affected by the outcome," demanding that the courts order the league to replay the game.

Although the suit was eventually dismissed, the day after it was filed the NFL officially admitted the noncall had been a mistake. A few months later, the league changed the replay review rules to allow coaches to challenge a failure to call pass interference. Perhaps predictably, this rule was interpreted extremely conservatively by officials. Thus another category of unreversed bad calls was created: failures to call pass interference when it had clearly occurred, but not quite clearly enough in the fickle judgment of the reviewing officials to warrant a reversal of the original noncall.

But the biggest problem with replay review isn't that it delays games or that it creates new gray zones of what constitutes a bad enough call to reverse or even that its application is inevitably arbitrary. From the perspective of deeply engaged fans, the most problematic aspect of replay review is that it creates a new set of barriers to fully experiencing the catharsis that is the most essential aspect of that experience.

Here is one of a potentially endless set of examples of why this is the case. In 1991, Michigan and Notre Dame met in Ann Arbor in another installment of one of the top rivalries in college football. Michigan was clinging to a three-point lead midway through the fourth quarter and faced a fourth and one at the Notre Dame 25. Rather than attempting a field goal, the team's coach, Gary Moeller, told his star receiver Desmond Howard that quarterback Elvis Grbac was going to throw him the ball, and he was going to catch it and score a touchdown. Howard agreed that this sounded like a good plan. A sideline microphone captured this conversation, which you can view on YouTube, as I have a few dozen times.

Facing Notre Dame's goal-line defense, Grbac faded back, pump faked a short pass to Howard, then lofted a long pass. The ball was overthrown, but Howard flew into a completely horizontal position and made an amazing catch a split second before hitting the ground just short of the back of the end zone The official's hands flew up to signal a touchdown, and complete bedlam ensued, both in the stadium and in front of millions of TV sets, including mine.

Today, that play would be reviewed, and indeed every fan would realize it was going to be reviewed almost before Howard hit the ground. There would be a several-minute delay while the referee huddled in front of a monitor and tried to determine whether the ball moved in Howard's hands when he and it hit the ground and which part of Howard's body was the first to contact the ground, and so on and so forth. It wouldn't be clear, or at least not absolutely so, from the initial replay whether the call on the field would stand. Thus, a moment of instantaneous ecstasy would be subjected to, as it were, pseudojudicial interruptus. And even if the call was upheld, some crucial aspect of the traditional experience would still have been altered and tainted by the obsessive—and ultimately futile—attempt to remove mistakes from the system. A moment of pure, instantaneous bliss—and of pure agony for the fans on the other side of the call— would have been lost to the demands of the iron cage of bureaucracy.

Is that cost worth incurring? That is the sort of ultimately aesthetic and psychological question that will have different answers for different people. For my part, I find it faintly ridiculous and more than a little annoying that close calls in football games now require a review process reminiscent of a federal appellate court hearing and only slightly less solemn.

On the other hand, now that fans have become accustomed to this process, going back to the good—or bad—old days is probably out of the question. So it will be increasingly the case that we older fans will remember enjoying or enduring what was in some ways a fundamentally different emotional experience of the game from that experienced by younger fans, for whom phrases such as "upon further review," and "indisputable visual evidence" will always have been as familiar as "beyond a reasonable doubt" and "you have the right to remain silent."

A MEANINGLESS GAME

Midway through the fourth quarter of the 1998 Rose Bowl, the guy sitting in front of me got up to purchase some nachos. The Wolverines were clinging to a precarious lead in a game they (we) needed to win to secure the first, and what will in all likelihood prove to be the only, national championship of my lifetime of Michigan football fandom. But to him, getting some nachos seemed like a more pressing matter than discovering whether the pinnacle of my experience as a fan would be triumph or disaster.

This, of course, was in no way surprising: on countless other occasions I have been the guy going to get the nachos while others were living and dying with every twist and turn of the action. (I'm reminded of doctors at a hospital having a casual and carefree conversation with each other as they head out to lunch, leaving in their wake patients to whom they have just delivered the most exhilarating or devastating news.) The overwhelming majority of the time, when I watch sports, my emotional engagement is shallow enough to make nachos sound at least potentially tasty, despite the fact that stadium food in general, and nachos in particular, tends to be pretty vile.

By contrast, during any big Michigan game, I'm no more capable of eating anything than I am of solving quadratic equations while drunk. I don't drink during Michigan games, either: the team needs my focus as a fan to be unimpaired by any mind-altering substance other than the game itself. For fans, deep engagement is a qualitatively different experience than "watching sports" in the generic sense, which is a form of consumption indistinguishable from other essentially passive and emotionally shallow leisure-time activities.

I'm constantly struck by this distinction in my own viewing: for instance, I'm watching, out of sheer habit and inertia, a very minor bowl game between Kansas State and Texas A&M, two teams to which I lack even the most attenuated connection, and, in the final minutes of the game, the camera focuses for a moment on a KSU fan with a look of utter distress grading into outright agony on her face. I think, for a moment, come on, this is a meaningless bowl game—how can you care this much? A moment later I recognize the absurdity of my reaction: as punishment for my insouciance, I will have the exact same look on my face a few days later, when Michigan is in the final minutes of a similarly meaningless bowl game.

Both these games were meaningless, in the sense that they had no bearing on anything that, before the season, the fans of these teams would have considered a meaningful outcome: that is, they had nothing to do with making the playoffs, or winning the conference, or even beating a hated rival. With the advent of the college football playoff, other bowl games are increasingly considered pointless postseason exhibitions—certainly that's how I think of any nonplayoff bowl game not involving Michigan. I will even stipulate, when I am not actually watching one, that, prior to 2021, all of Michigan's bowl games in recent years had been meaningless in this sense.

But with three minutes to go in that meaningless bowl game, I'm still going to have that look on my face.

The growing meaningless of nonplayoff bowl games has been thrown into sharp relief by the increasingly widespread practice of star players who are eligible for the coming spring's NFL draft choosing to sit these games out. Why, after all, risk injury in a meaningless game? Thus, for example, Stanford's star running back Christian McCaffrey announced a couple of weeks before his team's bowl game at the end of the 2016 season that he wouldn't be playing in it, triggering a heated debate between observers who praised the self-evident prudence of this decision and others who worried that this sort of prudence would be bad for college football, by which of course they meant college football fans.

But all games are meaningless, except to the extent that somebody cares about them. Professionals are paid to care, which is on some basic level antithetical to the emotional economy of the whole enterprise. Any deeply engaged fan can't help but notice how, immediately after even the most hotly contested and—for some portion of the audience—heartbreaking game, NFL players from the two teams will be exchanging cordial greetings, as they apparently laugh and joke about the agonizing experience to which some of them have just subjected their fans. This is completely natural behavior—after all, playing this game is their job—but it is still strangely discordant to the people who pay the bills.

The distinction between meaningful and meaningless games breaks down under the slightest pressure. The obliteration of that distinction by the profit motive is why gambling on sports is ultimately a profound perversion of any genuine rooting interest: reducing one's passion to mere pecuniary considerations is a species of emotional prostitution, which deeply engaged fans engage in at peril to their partisan souls. Indeed, the sudden open embrace, in the wake of the COVID pandemic, of sports gambling by the major American sports leagues has been one of the more disconcerting recent developments in the emotional economy of fandom.

Everyone suspects himself of at least one of the cardinal virtues, and this is mine: I have always been completely immune to the seductions of gambling. A friend has explained those charms to me like this: "When Michigan loses, they lost. When Michigan wins, we won. When I win money on a game, I won." That makes a certain twisted sense, and it may be that the passions experienced when one's team wins or loses are not so different from those that sports gamblers feel when their bets succeed or fail.

Still, in a way that feels uncomfortably cranky-old-mannish, I'm bothered by the passion with which the people who run big-time American sports have suddenly decided that the billions of dollars spent wagering on their games is a solution to various financial pressures. After years of listening to NFL TV broadcasters indulge in the occasional nudge nudge wink wink comment at the end of an otherwise decided game—"A lot of people are interested in this extra point, Phil!"—we have been thrust into a brave new world where the over/under is suddenly part of the graphic crawl, along with the scores and all the traditional stats.

When the thrill of victory has been transferred from the team to the current balance of your Internet sports bookmaking account, or the current standing of your fantasy football roster, something fundamental may have shifted. (Again, I wouldn't know.)

Still, people find meaning wherever they can. Perhaps as gambling becomes more ubiquitous among sports fans, the seductions of, on the one hand, deep engagement with one's team, and, on the other, wagering on its games, will for many fans come to seem more complementary than conflicting.

For my part, I will cling to what I imagine is the purity of my passion for Michigan football, uncontaminated by pecuniary considerations. (The mere thought of having real money riding on something that I already obviously care far too much about makes me almost literally queasy.) I can, I suspect, only afford one addiction at a time.

THE END OF THE WORLD AS WE KNOW IT

In 2017, the *New York Times* profiled Norman Podhoretz, focusing on his role in the New York literary scene of the 1950s and 1960s. Through the always treacherous lens of nostalgia, Podhoretz looks back fondly on the often vicious feuds of that era: "John Berryman, who was a friend of [Saul] Bellow's, came up to me—I didn't know who he was, this drunken guy—and he said, 'We'll get you for that review if it takes 10 years.' I was 23 years old. I go, 'What?'" The profile concludes on a melancholy note, as Podhoretz remarks that those days are long gone; nobody really argues about ideas much anymore. "All Americans really care about is sports," he says. "They pretend to care about other things, but what they care about is sports."

A cynical reader might respond that the implication of this claim—that what Americans should really care about are half-century-old literary feuds among New York intellectuals—is perhaps less than completely self-evident. A less cynical reader might acknowledge that Podhoretz has something of a point. Certainly, the attention we as a culture lavish on sports can seem more than a little excessive, given how relatively little attention we pay to more self-evidently important topics.

On the Michigan board, this point is driven home to us with relentless regularity by Cutter. A former career Navy officer, Cutter retired early. For years, Cutter's main interest on the board was future playing schedules. If you wanted to know if Michigan was really slated to play Arkansas nine years hence and Washington two years after that, or when the next game in Madison was likely to happen, Cutter was the go-to poster.

About fifteen years ago, however, Cutter's comprehensive research into scheduling questions began to take a back seat to a new interest: climate change. Soon, Cutter was writing about almost nothing else: a typical post came to consist of a series of copied and pasted stories about the science of climate change, with the invariable message that disaster was just around the corner if we as a society didn't take drastic action soon.

Initially, the board's reaction to this transformation was one of tolerant bemusement. After a time, however, other posters began to get annoyed. After all, wasn't he getting just a bit obsessive? (This question tended to be raised by people who would normally be arguing passionately about whether Anthony Carter was a better receiver than Desmond Howard.) Despite increasingly hostile blowback, Cutter was undeterred. Each month he would end up posting dozens of stories about climate change, until eventually the board pretty much stopped complaining about his weird fixation and just ignored him.

Then, about three years ago, a change took place. Not in Cutter, who if anything was posting with even more regularity about the imminent opening of the environmental Seventh Seal, but in the attitude of the board. At around the same time that the board's few open Trump supporters were more or less ostracized and chased off, it suddenly seemed to occur to the rest of us that maybe Cutter wasn't some sort of catastrophic alarmist but that climate change really was as severe a crisis as he had been claiming for all these years. People began to pose respectful questions to him about what the long-term consequences of climate change were for the future of the planet in general and Michigan football in particular. Cutter's most recent observations on this matter have been that we've only got about ten years left: after that, according to his estimates, college football as we know it is likely to cease to exist.

Michigan's football team will then become something akin to the University of Chicago's: a small-time operation, playing before a few thousand fans at most and traveling by bus to games only within a couple of hours drive. A society-wide realization that our economy is destroying the world will lead to such radical changes, as we suddenly grasp that our profligate ways are destroying the ecosystem.

Cutter's catastrophic environmentalism still elicits some mostly gentle mockery. Danny, the board's king of dry wit, has appointed himself the task of counting down how many Michigan football games are left before The End. But it seems that, deep down, most of the board has come to suspect that Cutter has been at least sort of right all along. What have we been doing, wasting our lives obsessing about questions such as when Michigan will finally beat Ohio State again, when the whole world now seems to be on the verge of burning?

The answer to that question isn't very satisfactory, of course. That answer consists, in the end, of admitting that there are almost always things that are more important than our particular passions, which by their nature are usually quite trivial in the broader scheme of things. Yet those passions are not trivial in at least one sense: they ultimately make us who we are.

The documentary film *Free Solo* chronicles rock climber Alex Honnold's quest to "free solo"—that is, to climb without the aid of climbing gear or ropes—El Capitan, a 3,200-foot rock wall in the Yosemite valley that took forty-two days to climb (with aid) the first time it was done, sixty years ago. Watching the film is a disorienting experience. What Honnold is attempting seems both completely impossible and completely crazy; even as we watch him go through with his quest, it seems like some sort of trick of computer-generated imagery, so outrageous is this feat that combines death-defying athleticism with extraordinary mental strength.

Honnold is in pursuit of a kind of perfection, which, if taken as seriously as he takes it, is something that always threatens to veer into a sort of madness. Indeed, the film portrays Honnold as a strange, enigmatic figure: a "dark soul," to use his own description of himself as a child. Obviously extremely intelligent—among other things free soloing at this level is a highly analytical activity—he is also surprisingly introspective about why he is living his life this way. (In his mid-thirties, he has spent his whole adult life literally living out of a van, pursuing good weather for climbs, although in recent years his feats have earned him what seems like a fair bit of money from equipment sponsors.)

It's a cliché that climbing is something that can inspire existential reflection, but in Honnold's case the reflection seems genuine, and tinged with a sort of pervasive melancholia. As he is about to launch his final assault on El Capitan, Honnold reflects on why he does what he does: "It's about being a warrior," he says. "It doesn't matter about the cause, necessarily. This is your path, and you will pursue it with excellence. You face your fear because your goal demands it. That is the goddamn warrior spirit."

Trying to climb a 3,200-foot sheer rock wall without a rope is in one sense an obviously absurd activity. So is, for that matter, trying to win drunken arguments about literary aesthetics with other intoxicated writers, or trying to do something about climate change by posting incessantly about it on a Michigan football message board, or writing a whole book obsessing about why people are so obsessed with what obsesses them.

All these things are in their own way absurd, and therefore all of them expose the pursuers of such passions to the risk that they will be ridiculed by those who don't share those particular passions. But still, we face our fear because our goal demands it. That is the goddam warrior spirit—even if the only battles we end up winning turn out to be virtual.

HOTEL CALIFORNIA

The night before the 2019 Michigan–Ohio State game, longtime board member EF Wolverine posted a mordant question: "Is anyone else crushed by an overwhelming sense of dread and despair about tomorrow?" He suggested, in apparent seriousness, that he "might self-medicate" so that he could "wake up tomorrow night, having missed the whole thing." At this point Michigan had lost seven straight meetings with its chief rival, and fourteen of the previous fifteen, in what is generally considered one of the half dozen most important rivalries in the sport.

From time to time a poster on the main Michigan and Ohio State boards will announce that he is taking the entire week of The Game off from work, since he wouldn't be able to get anything done anyway. This is not considered unusual or excessive behavior; rather, others respond that they are thinking of doing the same, or regretting that they cannot.

EF Wolverine's question received a less sympathetic response. While many posters acknowledged it was quite likely that tomorrow would be yet another disaster, admitting even thinking about avoiding the experience was treated as a sign of a contemptible moral cowardice. The most sympathetic response came from another longtime poster, JJ Walker:

> If you can't get excited tonight, you should literally give up sports. Just bet large on OSU and don't even watch the game. Don't watch any of

them, find some other hobby. Sports is an awful hobby for the woe-is-me crowd, you're just going to be disappointed 99% of the time when your team doesn't win it all.

JJ is an unusual poster in that he seems to have the rare capacity to be a deeply engaged fan who can nevertheless shrug off even the worst losses quickly. He genuinely loves sports in general, and rooting for Michigan in particular, but he somehow maintains a kind of balanced perspective that allows him to forget about a heartbreaking loss within half an hour instead of brooding about it for days or decades, like some people I know all too well. It's undoubtedly a much healthier attitude than that of the typical deeply engaged fan, but there's also something about it that seems somehow less than fully authentic. Let's face it: someone who gets over a breakup fast enough to be on Tinder half an hour later probably just wasn't that into you. The more you suffer, the more it shows you really care.

A far more common type of deeply engaged fan is one who claims that this is it, he can't take it anymore, and he's finally quitting Michigan football for good. In the end, this fan almost always discovers he just can't quit it—or the board, to which he will make an awkward return eventually. Shortly after that Ohio State game, which did turn out to be yet another excruciating loss, another poster announced that, while he wasn't necessarily getting a divorce, he would henceforth no longer invest any emotional energy in this ridiculously dysfunctional relationship. "I've sincerely stopped caring," his post was titled. "It 'helps' that I may not make it to another season as is but I don't really care either way. . . . The program is broken and nobody that can do anything about it will even try to do anything about it."

He went on to suggest that fans who still cared should put their money where their mouths are and stop buying tickets and official merchandise and making donations to the athletic department: "Do what you can and deem worth doing but do something other than bitch and get mad about it. That changes exactly zero. Nothing."

Me? I'm just kinda done. Again, doesn't really matter in my case but I've chosen to stop caring because it doesn't benefit me in any way. It

actively makes me feel angry and bad . . . and why do that to yourself?
UM Football used to be a fun escape and it just makes me angry now so
I finally decided to stop letting it. I don't accept what UM is. I won't be
putting my money in their pockets by donating, going to games or buying
merch (I will still donate to Mott's Children's Hospital). It's a drop in the
ocean but it's all I can do.

I don't blame anyone that thinks that's stupid, btw. Do what you like. I
just chose to stop caring and the program made that very easy for me to do.

But of course it doesn't really work that way. You can't really just
wake up one morning and "choose" to stop caring about something
that has been an integral part of your life, and therefore of your understanding of yourself—at least not without psychological mutila-
tion. Doing so is, at least in theory, an option, but this poster's dec-
laration, a few hours after yet another devastating loss, somehow
reminded me of a passage in Jim Bouton's *Ball Four* recounting how
his fellow pitcher Gary Bell would deal with a tough loss: "And then
sometimes, after a bad game, he'd sit in the back of the bus with five
or six beers in him and he'd mumble to himself, 'I don't give a shit. I
don't give a shit.' But he did."

How many times over the years have I seen a poster conclude he
has better things to do with his autumn Saturdays, and that all this
has finally become too much? The demand that people stop going
to games since that's the only thing the powers that be care about
or understand is also a standard part of these jeremiads. Almost all
these people discover that the board, like Michigan football itself,
is like the Hotel California: you can check out any time you like,
but you can never leave. A lifelong addiction to anything eventually becomes indistinguishable, for the addict, from the rhythm and
texture of life itself. Giving up your team, for the deeply engaged
fan, is like renouncing anything else that has become central to your
identity. Since November of 2016, I've contemplated for the first time
in my life under what circumstances I might choose to cease to be an
American. Choosing to cease to be a Michigan football fan does not
feel any less radical, in that either choice would require that I become
a fundamentally different person.

As time passes, I find that the passions that allow for the addiction of deep engagement narrow: when youth is on one's side, it's much easier to care deeply about many more things, including more sports teams. As a teenager, I felt real distress every time the Detroit Pistons and the Detroit Red Wings lost a game, which was often. Today I can barely name a single current member of either team, although I can recite their 1976 starting lineups from memory.

Like an alcoholic who discovers he can now drink only gin, I find only Michigan football can still elicit anything like the old thrill and despair. And there are days when I wonder, what if I should somehow cease to care about even that? Will I have at long last actually become a man, by putting away childish things? Or will at least a part of me remain a perpetual boy, who still gets upset—genuinely upset—about something as trivial, as fundamentally absurd, as who wins a college football game?

Given my age and social identity, being a deeply engaged college football fan is at least slightly embarrassing, like being a sixty-year-old man obsessed with *Star Wars* or *Harry Potter* or whether Prince What's-His-Name and his American bride are really going to move to Canada. Casual fandom, if one must be interested in sports at all, is much more respectable: at least it's something to make small talk about, like the weather. Being able to instantly cite the final score of every Michigan–Ohio State game of the 1970s is, by contrast, not the kind of accomplishment one should take pride in, if one wishes to be thought of as a Serious Person. But that is who people like us are, although we may choose to tactfully keep our less respectable passions out of sight in certain company.

Perhaps oddly, I've never felt the slightest urge to quit Michigan football, even after "we" stopped beating Ohio State, or winning conference championships every other year. I suspect this is how many people feel about their marriages, or their religion, or their country: they don't question their relationship to those things, because those things are what they themselves now are.

And it is better to be something than nothing, even if that something is not something other people really understand.

THE FLIGHT TRACKER

As far as Michigan football fans are concerned, this is the moment for which the Internet was invented. It is a few days before Christmas 2014, and for the past three weeks the board has been a nonstop frenzy, focused on one question, and one question alone: Who will be Michigan's next coach?

Now longtime poster Rockie has dropped a bombshell: a little birdie has told him that former Michigan quarterback Jim Harbaugh, currently one of the most successful coaches in the NFL, is coming home to Ann Arbor! For at least a few minutes, the entire board explodes in a kind of cyber Big Bang of universal ecstasy.

But that universe begins to cool rapidly. Newer posters, in particular, exhibit marked skepticism. Who exactly are Rockie's sources? How reliable are they? When will this be publicly announced? Why hasn't it been announced already? Are we being trolled? If this doesn't happen and we hire Greg Schiano, I swear I will never listen to another poster about anything like this ever again. And so on and so forth.

Rockie is a school bus driver in a small Ohio city. He used to be a roadie for the Christian heavy metal band Stryper. His writing style indicates he possesses a high school diploma at best, and his typical contribution to the board is photos of skanky bikini-clad pinup girls who look like pole dancers at the most depressing strip club you can possibly imagine. He also occasionally posts stories about how he evangelizes to some of the troubled teens he drives to and from school. He is not, in other words, the sort of source that most of the board—the typical member of which is an upper-class professional with a graduate degree—would consider a reliable authority on most subjects. But today, at least, this collection of doctors, lawyers, professors, journalists, etc., are hanging on his every word.

This is because we know that Rockie is very tight with a former Michigan linebacker, whose own father was the team's head coach in the early 1990s. The linebacker is now an NFL assistant coach, so he is, in this context, a truly connected guy. Rockie is our conduit to him; hence, we pore over every one of Rockie's not terribly literate utterances about the coaching search like Kabbalah scholars attempting to decode a sacred text.

In short, there is nothing like a coaching search to drive the online obsessions of already-obsessed fans to unparalleled heights. It makes the neuroses of game-day posting seem almost healthy by comparison. As long as the search lasts, every rumor or rank bit of pure speculation—not to mention any piece of actual information—will elicit paroxysms of joy and anguish, as posters fantasize about the potential a candidate has to fulfill our fondest dreams or bring about our worst nightmares. Each search, for the deeply engaged, follows a predictable initial trajectory. The cautious optimism that ruled when a search for a new coach seemed possible but not yet assured gives way, as soon as it becomes clear that the search is going to happen, to irrational exuberance. Inevitably, it will be reported (or more realistically, "reported") that Dream Candidate has been contacted by the athletic department and that he is most definitely interested.

The next stage is the Flight Tracker: various web tools that track airplane flights will be consulted for evidence that Dream Candidate may even now be flying our way for negotiations, or that our athletic director is headed his way. Posters who live near the airport will be implored to travel there to confirm Dream Candidate's actual arrival, and a couple will promise to do so.

Reports will surface that Dream Candidate's wife has been spotted house shopping in town. The contract, it seems, is all but signed. Then a couple of days pass, and nothing happens. At this point the community suffers a sudden collective loss of faith, and irrational exuberance gives way to extreme pessimism. Tales of previous search fiascos are repeated; those who were most certain that Dream Candidate was coming are mocked relentlessly, and indeed often mock themselves for their foolish optimism.

Over the next few days, names of less desirable candidates are floated, eliciting wails of frustration from many, along with calls for patience and realism from the—always heavily outnumbered—patient and realistic. Every bit of information and rumor is subjected to positively postmodern levels of hermeneutic analysis: perhaps this report of serious negotiations with Candidate A is merely a smoke screen, being leaked by the athletic department to deflect attention from the actual negotiations with Candidate B? Or maybe Candidate C is being pursued after all, given the fact that no evidence has emerged of any contact with him. That is, absence of evidence is indirect proof that attempts to keep the actual details of the search secret have been completely successful. Such casuistry ensures that every report can be interpreted both positively and negatively—and will be. Naturally, in this atmosphere of constant anxious uncertainty, the credentials of every putative source are subjected to the most exacting scrutiny. It's precisely because we know who Rockie's source is that board veterans are so elated by his news.

My brother—a professional historian—was wise enough to archive hundreds of board posts from December of 2014, and I'm struck by several things in them.

First, national sports journalists constantly published complete nonsense regarding the Michigan search. NFL journalists in particular reported with great confidence, over and over again, putative facts we now know were completely untrue, such as that Harbaugh had no interest in the Michigan job, or had already turned it down, etc.

Second, Rockie did in fact know exactly what was actually going on, even as ESPN talking heads with multimillion-dollar contracts ran their mouths on the basis of whatever false rumor had just tumbled into their unfastidious laps. Talk about fake news!

Third, the entire board spent almost the entire month having a collective nervous breakdown, as posters would oscillate between giddy optimism and dark despair, often within a matter of hours, if not minutes.

Looking even further back, I've found some notes I jotted down the last time Michigan hired the board's dream candidate, in December of 2007:

> We're going to end up with [LSU coach] Les Miles after all. Insiders on the "premium" boards—this means you have to pay ten bucks a month for your Internet information fix—are dropping broad hints that Something Big is in the works. . . . And then It Happens. Former Ohio State quarterback and current ESPN talking head Kirk Herbstreit announces on the morning of the SEC championship game that Miles will be Michigan's new coach, and that Georgia Tech defensive guru Jon Tenuta will be Miles' defensive coordinator!

I remember the moment these words came out of Herbstreit's mouth. I immediately call my friend Jon, who has small children and can't necessarily be watching ESPN nonstop on a Saturday morning. Jon is a nationally prominent journalist, who writes articles that can conceivably have a marginal effect on such questions as who will be the next president of the United States. But I know that he's far more interested in the question of who the next head football coach of the University of Michigan will be. He is a huge fan of both Miles and Tenuta, and when I tell him the news he almost breaks down and weeps with happiness.

Yet within minutes of Herbstreit's announcement, a premium board is reporting disturbing news. It appears that ESPN has jumped the gun, and by doing so has jeopardized whatever negotiations are going on! Message boards across the Internet metaphorically explode with rage and anxiety. It's noted darkly that a former OSU quarterback is ruining Michigan's coaching search, and more than one poster pledges to take some terrible vengeance. As the hours on this grim day pass, extremely disquieting rumors begin to circulate. It's hinted that Michigan athletic director Bill Martin had been out of cell phone range during the most crucial negotiating period, on his sailboat off the coast of Florida. This sounds like nothing but the most extreme board paranoia—yet incredibly, over the next few days this story is more or less confirmed. Meanwhile, Les Miles is holding a press conference to announce he's signing a contract extension with LSU and has no plans to coach anywhere else. Some Michigan fans study the exact language Miles uses with extreme care and conclude that what he's really saying is that he's still interested in the Michigan job.

By that night, Michigan Internet Nation is in something close to despair. It appears we had every chance to hire our dream coach, but our utterly incompetent-in-over-his-head-doesn't-really-know-anything-about-sports athletic director has destroyed our one chance to do so. Over the next week, mordant references to *Gilligan's Island* ("a three-hour tour") clog servers. By the weekend, things reach rock bottom when a credible source on a premium board hints that Brady Hoke—an undistinguished Mid-American Conference coach, whose only real qualification is that he's a friend of current Michigan coach Lloyd Carr—is now a leading candidate. Howls of outrage ring out on every Michigan site.

The Brady Hoke Threat passes. Over the next few days, stories circulate that Michigan is meeting with Greg Schiano, Rutgers' head coach and in most peoples' eyes a good if not great prospect. Hopes rise, sort of, along with lots of complaints about Schiano's evident weaknesses. Are we really settling for Greg Schiano? The answer is soon revealed to be no—Schiano turns down the job. Other names pop up, such as Jim Grobe, Wake Forest's coach, whose main qualification seems to be a jut-jawed profile, like what Hollywood thinks a coach should look like, plus one outstanding season at Wake Forest—a school, apologists for his candidacy remind us, that has something like a total of 374 male students, most of whom are Baptist ministers in training.

The search reaches the stage where it has sunk in for everyone, even the most optimistic, that hiring a coach is hard. Apparently, unlike the average Michigan poster, desirable candidates can easily imagine why they might not take the job.

At this point, most board mavens are hoping the search comes to a halt for another four weeks or so, until Les Miles has won his national championship at LSU and Bill Martin (or Martin's successor after the university's president, Mary Sue Coleman, hands him a richly deserved pink slip) goes out and hires him anyway, contract extension be damned. What a coup that will be—hiring the man who will just have destroyed OSU's national championship dreams yet again!

But most of us realize that, at this point, this is more of a fantasy than a realistic plan. After all, there are grave doubts about whether Martin ever really wanted to hire Miles, plus rumors persist that Miles did something that has left him on permanently bad terms with Lloyd Carr. Some posters even begin to flirt with the wacky idea of hiring an interim coach for a season and trying again next year.

Yet, just as things seem their darkest, news leaks out on Friday afternoon that, even at this very moment, Coleman and Martin are meeting at a hotel in Toledo, Ohio, with West Virginia coach Rich Rodriguez! Rodriguez is universally considered a grade A candidate, but because he turned down Alabama just last year and signed a big contract extension at that time, his name has hardly been raised over the course of the last frantic month.

Instantly, all the main Michigan and West Virginia boards are again thrown into a frenzy. Fans pore over every scrap of official information about the meeting, analyzing, interpreting, and deconstructing. The many rumors about what's going on get even more obsessive treatment. On the Michigan boards, the bona fides of supposed WVU "insiders" posting on the Mountaineer boards are examined with the care squinty-eyed jewelers apply to dubious lapidary specimens. The words of one poster in particular, with the peculiar handle "Eerhole," are considered worthy of the closest attention.

A year ago, Eerhole stated confidently that Rodriguez was staying at West Virginia rather than taking the megabucks offer from Alabama. Because it was widely assumed at the time that Rodriguez would take the Alabama offer, Eerhole's credibility is high. Now he's posting the news that Rodriguez has turned down Michigan's offer. A wave of despair sweeps over the Wolverine boards. The coaching search has been going on for nearly a month, and, after a series of constant twists and missteps, having one of the top half dozen coaches suddenly dangled before us and then just as suddenly yanked away has left us almost sick with frustration and dread.

For my brother and me, the morning is made worse by the extraordinarily bad luck that, at this precise moment, we're trapped at an Important Family Function. My brother's wife, who is all too familiar with our Michigan football fetish, has threatened us with dire consequences if we attempt to use our cell phones to establish contact with the outside world during the ceremony, which is interminable. Finally, we're released from bondage, and we sprint out of the church into the cold Colorado air, where the cellular reception is better. Frantic calls soon convey the exhilarating news—no less an authority than Eerhole himself has posted a despairing message on the West Virginia board! That's all the confirmation we need. The Rich Rodriguez era has unofficially begun.

The denouement of this story is less inspiring: Dream Candidate Rodriguez turned out to be a total disaster, and after three seasons was replaced by none other than Brady Hoke, the onetime worst-case scenario hire. Hoke's resume had improved only marginally in the interim, and, far less surprisingly, he also proves to be a disaster. Hoke was hired by new athletic director Dave Brandon, a pompous idiot who ignored Hoke's mediocre record because he was impressed by Hoke in a one-on-one interview. (Social science has established that one-on-one job interviews are useless for determining anything other than whether the interviewer likes the candidate.)

Brandon himself turned out to be an even bigger disaster than either Rodriguez or Hoke—among other things he sent abusive replies to hundreds of fans who had the temerity to email him even the politest complaints—to the point where more than one thousand students marched on the university president's residence, demanding his firing. After he was fired, Brandon was named CEO of Toys "R" Us, which he promptly drove into bankruptcy. (The meritocracy!)

The hiring of yet another dream candidate in 2014 has to this point produced a much more mixed result: Jim Harbaugh has done far better than Rodriguez and Hoke but has still been a disappointment relative to the sky-high expectations that greeted his arrival. Now some board posters are pining for yet another coaching search, although all but the most irrational must recognize that the odds of such a process producing an improvement are slim at best.

Nevertheless, at some point we will again be tracking flights and picking apart Internet rumors, as we look to a future that seems once again full of infinite possibilities.

AN ACUTE LIMITED EXCELLENCE

One of the more melancholy moments in that melancholy classic *The Great Gatsby* takes place when Nick Carraway gets together with his former Yale classmate Tom Buchanan. Tom is introduced to the reader as "one of the most powerful ends that ever played football at New Haven." Tom, Nick relates, "was a national figure in a way, one of those men who reach such an acute limited excellence at twenty-one that everything afterward savors of anti-climax." A better description of the inherent pathos of the life of the former star athlete is difficult to imagine.

Now, a decade after his exploits on the field, Tom is very rich—in proper Gilded Age fashion, he has inherited his money—and very bored, and he and his wife Daisy are living aimless lives:

> Why they came East I don't know. They had spent a year in France, for no particular reason, and then drifted here and there unrestfully wherever people played polo and were rich together.... I felt that Tom would drift on forever seeking, a little wistfully, for the dramatic turbulence of some irrecoverable football game.

Although Fitzgerald is one of the most written-about American authors, and his fascination with college football, and more specifically the Princeton Tigers, has been noted by critics, the possible role he played in bringing about a crucial strategic innovation that shaped the modern game of football was, until recently, overlooked. Fitzgerald attended the 1911 Harvard–Princeton game, a few weeks after his fifteenth birthday. Princeton scored a last-minute touchdown to defeat their archrival. According to his biographers, Fitzgerald decided that very afternoon that he would enroll at the school.

Two autumns later he did. He tried out for the football team and was cut on the first day of practice. Many scholars believe this event haunted Fitzgerald and that it helped inspire the fascination with failure and rejection that is a prominent feature of much of his writing in general, and *The Great Gatsby* in particular.

Fitzgerald was, even for his time, a small man—as an undergraduate he weighed only 135 pounds—and he had been an undistinguished high school football player in Minnesota, so his deep disappointment at failing to make the roster of what was one of the elite college teams of the era seems all out of proportion to the plausibility of that ambition. Still, this sort of disappointment, as Fitzgerald's writing often reminds us, is rarely connected to whether the dream was ever plausible.

Nevertheless Fitzgerald remained positively obsessed with Princeton football for the rest of his short life. This aspect of his personality has been given short shrift by many of his biographers: as Kevin Helliker argued in a fascinating 2014 essay, the story of Fitzgerald's devotion to the Princeton team, unlike his better-known obsessions with alcohol, women, jazz, and money, "never fit well in the narrative of Fitzgerald as a tortured artist, heartbroken by his wife's mental illness and confronted at every turn by commercial failure."

Yet little if anything mattered to the great writer more than the fortunes of Princeton football. Helliker unearthed a 1956 interview in the *Michigan Daily*, the University of Michigan's student newspaper, with Fritz Crisler, Michigan's football coach in the 1940s. Before coming to Ann Arbor, Crisler had coached Princeton from 1932 through 1937. Today, Crisler is best remembered as the inventor of the platoon system: the practice of using different sets of players on offense and defense. Helliker speculates, on the basis of somewhat tenuous but all the more tantalizing evidence, that the great novelist himself may have inspired Crisler's enormously important innovation.

The 1956 interview was conducted by Donald Yates, a graduate student in romance languages. Yates—who knew little about football other than that Fitzgerald loved the game—asked a question that apparently Crisler had never been asked before, at least for print: Had he ever talked to Fitzgerald about Princeton football when Crisler had been the team's coach? Had he ever.

Fitzgerald, Helliker argues, was "a pioneer of the fanaticism that characterizes so many college football fans today, and his relationship with Crisler was exhibit one." This fanaticism manifested itself in Fitzgerald's habit of phoning Crisler on the Friday nights before games to regale the coach with his ideas about how to achieve victory. These late-night phone calls—usually between midnight and six in the morning, from cities all over the country—often came, in Crisler's recollection, amid "the laughter and cries of a dying party," which sounds like a detail straight out of one of the novelist's books.

Crisler was struck by the manic intensity of Fitzgerald's devotion. "It wasn't just a matter of the habitual old grad spirit and enthusiasm," he told Yates. "There was something beyond comprehension in the intensity of his feelings. Listening to him unload his soul as many times as I did, I finally came to the conclusion that what Scott felt was really an unusual, a consuming devotion to the Princeton football team."

Fitzgerald's enthusiasm was reflected in his eagerness to share with Crisler—already one of the most famous college football coaches in the country—his strategic and tactical ideas. (Imagine trying this with Nick Saban or Dabo Swinney today.) And Crisler listened. "Sometimes he had a new play or strategy he wanted me to use," Crisler told Yates. "Some of the ideas Scott used to suggest to me over the phone were reasonable—and some were fantastic." One of those suggestions, Crisler said, involved "a scheme for a whole new offense. Something that involved a two-platoon system."

Sadly, for people who are fans of both college football and F. Scott Fitzgerald, Donald Yates was himself only a fan of the latter. So it did not occur to him to ask what would have been, from a fan's perspective, the natural follow-up: Did Crisler specifically get his idea for platoon football from none other than the author of *The Great Gatsby*? Nearly sixty years later, when Helliker interviewed Yates, Yates agreed that this seemed to be what Crisler had been saying.

The indefatigable Helliker unearthed one more suggestive piece of evidence: a 1962 biography of Fitzgerald by Andrew Turnbull that recounts how a Princeton athletic manager during Crisler's tenure got a call from Fitzgerald, advocating that Princeton use two sets of players on offense: "One will be big—all men over two hundred pounds. This team will be used to batter them down and wear them out. Then the little team, the pony team [the Fitzgeralds?], will go in and make the touchdowns."

Helliker's narrative ends on an appropriately somber note. It's well known that Fitzgerald was reading a copy of the *Princeton Alumni Weekly* when he was struck down by his fatal heart attack. What few of even the most fanatical acolytes of Fitzgerald fandom know is that he was reading the magazine's analysis of the football team's prospects for the coming season.

"In the margins of that newsletter," Helliker notes, "Fitzgerald had scribbled several comments, including 'good prose'—which makes college football the last thing he ever wrote about."

Fitzgerald was twenty-seven years old when he wrote *The Great Gatsby*. The whole book is pervaded by a sense that the passions and conquests of youth are fleeting, that life is passing away, and that the good times may well be gone for good:

> I was thirty. Before me stretched the portentous menacing road of a new decade. . . .
>
> Thirty—the promise of a decade of loneliness, a thinning list of single men to know, a thinning briefcase of enthusiasm, thinning hair. But there was Jordan beside me who, unlike Daisy, was too wise ever to carry well-forgotten dreams from age to age. . . .
>
> So we drove on toward death through the cooling twilight.

Athletes suffer the indignities of age sooner than most of us, which is surely one reason why Fitzgerald found his creation's doomed search for the dramatic turbulence of a college football game so emblematic. It's a hell of a thing to achieve your signal moment of greatness at twenty-one—much like a man who one day discovers that he wrote the great American novel when he was still in his mid-twenties, and that everything afterward was going to savor of anticlimax.

DUENDE

Even for the most deeply engaged fans, sports are, most of the time, more than a little boring. We sit in the rain and the snow, we bake in the sun, we sink deeper into the couch, remote in hand, waiting for something to happen that will make the countless hours we've wasted on this thing of ours seem worthwhile, as opposed to the unpleasant combination of the tedious, the neurotic, and the excruciating that makes up the great bulk of our fandom. And then . . .

Michigan Stadium, October 27, 1979. In the middle of what will end up being the second-worst season in Bo Schembechler's twenty-one-year tenure as Michigan's coach, the Wolverines are struggling to defeat perennial doormat Indiana. Indeed, with just six seconds left, the game is tied. Michigan has the ball at the Indiana 45, with time for one more play.

This is in the days before college football instituted overtime, so the game seems almost certain to end in a tie—a terrible result for a Michigan team that, by 2019, will have defeated the Hoosiers in thirty-eight of thirty-nine meetings. Is there such a thing as deeply engaged Indiana football fans? In a world of almost unimaginably exotic passions—just open your web browser—it stands to reason that there must be. Still, is some minimal possibility of winning something important a prerequisite for a team to attract more than a handful of particularly freakish masochists to the realms of deeply engaged fandom?

Quarterback John Wangler drops back to pass, but not before, absurdly, performing a play action fake handoff to the tailback. (The state of Michigan's passing offense in those days was practically Neo-lithic.) With a defensive lineman in his face, he throws the wobbly ball over the middle to freshman receiver Anthony Carter, who is running a 25-yard post route. Carter, who is listed at 161 pounds but would probably only tip the scales at that weight if he were holding a bowling ball, is almost immediately hit around the ankles of his gazelle-like legs by a diving Indiana defensive back.

For an instant he is knocked off his feet, and his body is momen-tarily at a 45-degree angle to the ground as he hurtles toward the goal line. The laws of physics pretty much dictate that he has to fall down at this point, but somehow he magically regains his balance before eluding a final desperate diving tackle by an Indiana safety, who is left face down on the turf clutching at air. Arms raised, knees pump-ing high, he crosses the goal line and into history, in what remains forty-plus years later the most famous final play in the 140-year story of Michigan football.

I am one hundred miles away, listening to all this on the radio, where the scene is being narrated by Bob Ufer, Michigan's legendary announcer. Ufer, who improbably enough set the world record in the indoor quarter-mile run when competing for Michigan thirty-seven years earlier, is famous for broadcasts that in no way disguise his frankly unhinged passion. Among other things, he honks a horn every time Michigan scores—one honk per point. The horn began its career on the combat jeep General George Patton—the very man who famously declared that America would never lose a war because we hate losing so much—rode while leading the Third Army through Europe in World War II. (Patton willed it to his nephew, who later gave it to Ufer.)

His call of Carter's touchdown goes like this: "Under center is Wangler at the 45, he goes back, he's looking for a receiver, he throws downfield to Carter, Carter, Carter..." He then becomes completely incoherent, before unleashing a scream of ecstasy or agony remi-niscent of Robert Plant's bone-chilling eldritch wail near the end of

"Since I've Been Loving You." For several seconds afterward, my radio features nothing but crowd noise. Only then does Ufer recover enough composure to let his audience know that never in his thirty-five years of covering Michigan football has he seen anything like this.

"This" is that moment of transcendent experience—as likely, or more likely, to be of pain as joy—that the deeply engaged fan pursues, while enduring what sometimes seem like endless stretches of boring banality. What we seek are those dark ecstatic moments that, in art, have been described as the arrival of the duende.

In his "Theory and Play of the Duende," Federico García Lorca says this:

> In all Arab music, dance, song or elegy, the arrival of duende is greeted with vigorous cries of "Allah! Allah!" so close to the "Ole!" of the bullfight, and who knows whether they are not the same? And in all songs of Southern Spain, the appearance of the duende is followed by sincere cries of: "Viva Dios!" deep, human, tender cries of communication with God, through the five senses, thanks to the duende that shakes the voice and body of the dancer. . . .
>
> Years ago, an eighty-year-old woman came first in a dance contest in Jerez de la Frontera, against lovely women and girls with liquid waists, merely by raising her arms, throwing back her head, and stamping her foot on the floor: but in that crowd of muses and angels with lovely forms and smiles, who could earn the prize but her moribund duende sweeping the earth with its wings made of rusty knives.

Lorca calls the duende (the Spanish word literally means a small, ghostlike creature) "a mysterious force that everyone feels and no philosopher has explained." The Australian singer Nick Cave explains: "All love songs must contain duende. For the love song is never truly happy. It must first embrace the potential for pain."

That is a perfectly concise description of the essence of fandom.

Not long ago, I saw Anthony Carter at a Michigan game, standing alone on the sidelines. We have almost exactly the same birthday; and on some level I found it difficult to believe that this stout figure on the edge of old age could be the same ethereal being who, when I was a college student in Ann Arbor, was the most compelling athlete I had ever seen, and—had I but known it—would ever see. Carter was someone who, every time he touched the ball, made you believe you might be about to see something dark, mysterious, and in some way magical. Like certain artists and athletes, he had duende, which is not something that can be described: it can only be felt.

Now he is an ordinary man, like any other. I miss him, and I imagine he does too.

A SEASON WITHOUT SPORTS

Six months into the pandemic, sports are finally back, more or less. Indeed in one sense they're more present than ever: by mid-September, Major League Baseball, the NBA, the NFL, and the NHL are, for the first time, playing their seasons simultaneously, although before mostly empty stands. That emptiness—spectator sports without spectators—lends a surreal air to the games, to the point where they seem not quite legitimate, but rather more like desperate artificial spectacles for desperate times. The leagues try to compensate for the absence of fans by piping in crowd noise or placing cardboard cutout figures in the seats most often scanned by the television cameras. These devices just end up adding to the fantastical flavor of the proceedings.

By contrast, my favorite team and sport still find themselves on the horns of a cruel dilemma. On the one hand, canceling the college football season altogether seems impossible from a fiscal perspective. College sports in America are a multibillion-dollar enterprise—and that enterprise is, as a practical matter, completely dependent on the money that comes from playing college football. Hence, six months into what is shaping up as the worst pandemic in the nation's history, the talk is not of whether the sport will be played this year, but when and how. Not surprisingly, the Southeastern Conference—the home of the top teams in the country's most football-crazed region—led the charge over the summer to play some sort of modified season, and the other major conferences soon began to follow suit. Whether or not other students end up staying on campus, whether or not the games will feature any actual fans in the stands, whether or not the pandemic is still raging, whether or not the games might have to be moved to late in the fall, or even the winter, the message from the sport's power brokers has been that, one way or another, college football has to happen. Otherwise, everybody will go broke.

On the other hand, the outrageousness of playing college football on campuses where most if not all students have been prohibited from attending class in person—indeed, at a number of schools, many students have already been sent home, as it becomes ever more evident that residential universities are veritable petri dishes for COVID transmission—is so flagrant that even some administrators who have grown accustomed to shutting their eyes to all the sport's hypocrisies and inequities continue to hesitate to actually go forward with the season. The Big Ten in particular—as always, priding itself on its supposed commitment to academic values—finds it difficult to convince enough of its university presidents to give their blessing, despite the extreme financial risk. Indeed in August the conference announces that it is, for the time being, canceling the entire season.

As September crawls along, however, stories emerge that the conference is considering playing some sort of schedule beginning in January, despite the fact that much of the upper Midwest features subarctic conditions during the first two months of the year. Then word comes that perhaps the Big Ten will begin playing around Thanksgiving, or even earlier. Finally, an announcement is made that a truncated eight-game schedule will start in late October, with games featuring no fans other than the players' families.

The board, deprived for the first time in its twenty-five-year existence of its regular autumn intoxicant, is, somewhat surprisingly, essentially split on the question of whether the season should happen at all. Apparently many of even the most deeply engaged fans find the idea of their beloved team playing under these conditions—with protests in the streets, the economy in collapse, the Trump administration's authoritarianism becoming ever more overt, and most of all, no sign of the pandemic abating—too absurd to countenance.

Although I myself remain deeply ambivalent on the question, I find this resistance to our collective addiction in the name of trying to behave like responsible citizens, instead of hopeless addicts, ultimately rather encouraging. Still, I discover that, in the midst of all the horror and chaos, I really want to go back to Michigan Stadium.

As the September light and the first scents of fall fill the air, I find myself overwhelmed with a sense of visceral nostalgia—not for another Michigan football season, per se, which remains for the moment a pallid abstraction—but for the simple experience of attending a real Michigan game, and everything that goes with it, including fans. To meet my fellow fanatics for food and drink and conversation at the tailgate before the game; to sit squeezed together with 110,000 of my closest friends in the stands; to walk back to the sound of crunching leaves under our feet afterward, reveling in the victory or lamenting the loss—my memories of having done these things on countless occasions suddenly conjure up, more powerfully than anything has up until now, a longing for the Before Time.

I realize that, in the grand scheme of things, not being able to attend a college football game is a trivial matter, when so many people have lost so much more. Indeed, I understand that we are at the moment just weeks away from an election that might well determine whether America slides for the foreseeable future into unambiguous authoritarianism. I know all this well enough—and yet, at this moment, I want more than anything else to experience this one thing that has played such an inexplicably big role in my emotional life.

"You only do two days," the inmates of our prisons supposedly tell each other, "that first day and that last day." Perhaps we prisoners of the pandemic should think of this time in the same way. And so I wait for that last day—and for another day that will come sometime after it, when I will be able to walk through the dark and narrow tunnel, into the sunlight illuminating the immense stadium before me, transformed once again by the longing of exile into the awe-inspiring sight it was on the day I first saw it as a child.

TANGLED UP
IN BLUE

The news broke late Saturday morning, exactly thirty-seven minutes prior to kickoff.

Ever since Tuesday night, Michigan football had barely merited a mention on the board, despite the fact that we were now heading into the third game of the long-delayed season. Tuesday itself had turned into the political equivalent of the biggest of big games: the almost unbearable anticipation with which the day began, usually expressed as either nervous confidence in victory, or open dread of defeat; the celebration, early in the evening's proceedings, of every hopeful sign; the sudden collapse of faith as soon as things began to go badly; the bitter lamentations of pessimists—and, per usual, as soon as things began to go badly almost everyone instantly became a pessimist—regarding the overconfidence that had been everywhere just an hour earlier.

Election night, in other words, was exactly like the board during the Ohio State game, at least back when Michigan actually used to beat Ohio State sometimes. By an organic process of shaming and shunning, the board had by now been purged of all open Trump supporters, so election night was an unambivalently partisan experience, but in regard to something that even the most hopelessly obsessive Michigan fan still realized was almost infinitely more important than any football game.

Still, the manic swings of emotion on display were indistinguishable from the agony and the ecstasy of the normal, or more accurately abnormal, game-day board. The most striking of these was what board denizen Michael Elkon has described to me as the psychology of the "banked win." A banked win happens when as a psychological matter fans treat a game as already won, even though the contest isn't actually over. This of course creates the possibility of the most painful of all losses: the revocation of that win. Elkon offers the example of Atlanta leading New England by 28–3 in the Super Bowl. Atlanta fans were understandably, but oh so recklessly, already celebrating that championship, only to see it snatched away in a kind of slow-motion nightmare.

By 10 p.m. or so on Tuesday, the same scenario seemed to be unfolding on the board, as Biden's victory over Trump—which almost all of us had, as a psychological matter, come to treat as a foregone conclusion—he was up by 10 percentage points in the national polls!—was suddenly in serious peril. This would be the most painful possible reversal of a banked win, except what would be lost wouldn't be a football game: it would, quite possibly, mark the practical disappearance of what we considered to be America.

By Wednesday morning, when it was finally clear that, despite the unspeakable agonies of Tuesday night, Donald Trump almost certainly wasn't going to be re-elected after all, the board's attention turned to the official calling of the race by the media. As the weekend approached, the major media's refusal to declare Biden the winner created ever-increasing frustration, along with a healthy dose of paranoia. We won! Why won't they call it? *Are they somehow going to manage to steal this thing?* Meanwhile, the fact that Michigan had a game on Saturday was practically forgotten—an impossibility in normal times.

By Saturday morning the frustration is boiling over, and crowding out the handful of posts that attempt to discuss the Indiana game that is about to kick off. Michigan had beaten Indiana twenty-four straight times and had lost only once to the Hoosiers since LBJ was president. Now if we had been paying attention we would have noticed that they actually looked suspiciously good this season. But we weren't.

Then at 11:23 Eastern Standard Time, the news is posted by multiple posters, within seconds of it being news: CNN has called the race!

Moments later, the other major networks follow suit. The explosion of joy on the board can be compared only to the moment when Cougar quarterback Ryan Leaf's attempt to stop the clock by spiking the ball on the last play of the 1998 Rose Bowl failed, ensuring a perfect season and a national championship for our beloved Wolverines.

Grown men admit they are weeping with relief, and I think of a post from BigLake on Election Eve:

> It's truly affirming and inspiring to have a common forum with progressive, smart, honest people, who all happen to have come together under the banner of Michigan football (frankly that's so freaking far in the rearview it's diminished to a speck). But really, the common thread for most posters on this board is decency, and the undying will to do right by our family and friends. If there are two words that unite us more than "Go Blue," then they're most certainly "Fuck Trump."

Minutes later it's kickoff time, and almost instantly the board is transformed into its normal maelstrom of game-day misery, which turns out to be fully warranted on this particular afternoon, as Michigan is routed by an Indiana team that never ever beats "us." Yet after the three and a half hours of nonstop masochistic wailing subsides, even the most cynical and pessimistic posters admit that it really doesn't seem to matter much at the moment: after all, "we" have won the only game that really counts.

Or not the only game: within forty-eight hours the news comes that a highly effective vaccine against the COVID-19 virus has been developed, which signals that even more effective vaccines are likely on the way. As Thanksgiving approaches, the board is taking what is shaping up as a truly catastrophic Michigan football season in very uncharacteristic stride.

It seems the trials of a plague year may be helping a bunch of mostly middle-age men to grow up just a little—although if, or rather when, we lose to Ohio State again in a few weeks by some gruesome score, that newfound equanimity will no doubt be annihilated, at least temporarily. (The Game actually ends up being canceled by the pandemic forty-eight hours before the scheduled kickoff. The relief

I feel at hearing this news—from a twentysomething grocery clerk wearing an OSU jersey, who noticed my Michigan hat—is one of the more sobering moments of a dire year.)

But for now at least, politics and medicine are allowing our community of inveterate masochists to revel in the joyful sight of Nike beating back Nemesis. Perhaps there is light at the end of the long dark tunnel of this plague year after all.

THE CIRCLE GAME

Much of this book has been dedicated to complaining, about sports, sports fans, the Internet, plutocracy, consumerism, authoritarianism, inequality, and much more besides. Let's face it, there's a lot to complain about at the moment. Like all people, we were born at a bad time.

And, the world being what it is, I could continue in this vein pretty much indefinitely. For instance, the last major sports event that took place before all the games suddenly went away was, appropriately enough, American sports' ultimate Big Game. The Super Bowl represents almost everything that's most obnoxious about big-time sports in this country. A grotesque amalgam of pomposity (each game is assigned a Roman numeral, and the coin flip alone is accompanied by a level of ceremony appropriate to the investiture of a pope), commercialism (the media breathlessly "rank" the commercials broadcast during the game, at a cost of $11 million per minute), militaristic nationalism (a flag approximately the size of Rhode Island is usually unfurled before kickoff, while a screaming comes across the sky in the form of a couple billion dollars' worth of Air Force equipment), and unabashed worship of the celebrity-entertainment complex (the halftime show invariably makes a Las Vegas revue seem tastefully understated), the whole spectacle is an advertisement for so many awful things about a culture which specializes in advertising its awfulness in the most garish ways possible.

I watched it though. Why? Because on some level, despite all their undeniable awfulness, I still care about sports, and everything they've meant and still mean to me after a half century of caring about them.

A few days earlier, former NBA superstar Kobe Bryant had been killed in a helicopter crash. Bryant's death elicited an astonishing outpouring of what seemed to be genuine grief among an enormous number of people who, with very few exceptions, did not know Bryant personally. For example, many board posters grappled with the extent to which Bryant's death shook them. This, predictably, led some other posters to wonder why Bryant's death produced such strong reactions, especially given a great deal of evidence suggesting that Bryant committed a violent sexual assault on a young woman and then bought his way out of legal jeopardy. The district attorney who prosecuted the case against Bryant is a former student of mine, and both the facts and the allegations in the case make for extremely disturbing reading.

One of the board's moderators lodged a passionate complaint:

Kobe was a shitty person who happened to be good at sports. The deification of him is odd. This is one of the more pragmatic and reasonable places I post online, and even here most of you are like, "Omigod, only say nice things!" I don't get it. I have no problem remembering the guy as a great athlete, but pointing out he was very likely a rapist who bought his way out of prosecution is very much part of the story of who he was.

Another of the board's longest-term residents responded this way:

It's not really deification of sports figures—for many it's more like what Don Draper spoke about regarding the power of nostalgia. So many great memories are associated with watching sports icons, including those you may have shared with your dad, or your friends, or others. So when they leave us—well—it can be really fucking sad.

This was a reference to the scene in the television series *Mad Men* in which the advertising guru Don Draper pitches the idea to Kodak executives of calling their slide projector wheel a "carousel." Draper explains:

My first job was in-house at a fur company, with this old-pro copywriter, a Greek named Teddy. Teddy told me that the most important idea in advertising is "new." It creates an itch. You simply put your product in there as a kind of calamine lotion. But he also talked about a deeper bond with the product: Nostalgia. It's delicate, but potent.

Draper then starts a slideshow on Kodak's projector. This consists of photographs of various joyful moments he has shared with his wife and his children, during what we the television audience know were better times than the all-too-fraught present. As the images of a once-happy family flicker by, he says:

> Teddy told me that in Greek, "nostalgia" literally means "the pain from an old wound." It's a twinge in your heart far more powerful than memory alone. This device isn't a spaceship. It's a time machine. It goes backwards, forwards, takes us to a place where we ache to go again. It's not called the wheel. It's called the carousel. It lets us travel the way a child travels. Round and around, and back home again, to a place we know we are loved.

Fandom, too, is a kind of time machine. If this book were longer it would have talked about sitting absolutely alone in the 101,701-seat Michigan Stadium in June of 1985, back in the days when you were allowed to do that kind of thing without threatening national security, feeling the summer breeze and gazing down at the field, remembering.

It would have described being in the stands with 93,848 other fans at the 2004 Rose Bowl, as a great USC team was dominating a good but not good enough Michigan side, and, as any last hope of victory slipped away in the fourth quarter, suddenly noticing the deep purple dusk enveloping the San Gabriel Mountains beyond the stadium's rim and letting the beauty of that panorama take some of the bad feeling away.

It would have captured the simple pleasure of a golf nap, when you fall asleep in front of the TV on a lazy summer Sunday afternoon to the dulcet sounds of Jim Nantz's eternally soothing voice. It's probably not possible to sound happier than Nantz sounds when he's interviewing a rich old white guy about what an amazing job the tournament's corporate sponsor has done again this year.

This book could have recounted setting a 12-inch portable TV on top of a Chevy Suburban in a driveway in Kalamazoo, Michigan, eighty miles from South Bend, Indiana, in order to pull in, barely, a fuzzy telecast of the 1980 Michigan–Notre Dame game, which, because of the absurd rules governing such things at the time, was broadcast only on the South Bend station. And it would have described the end of that game, when Tony Hunter caught a pass on the last play from scrimmage while standing with one foot out of bounds, which gained the Irish exactly enough yardage so that Harry Oliver's 51-yard game-winning field goal could just crawl over the crossbar. Legend has it that the wind in Oliver's face mysteriously ceased just as his foot connected with the ball. Afterward, someone told Oliver that every woman on campus would want to be with him that evening, and he replied, there's only one woman for me, and that's Our Lady. Cancer would carry him away at the age of forty-seven. RIP Harry Oliver.

It would have talked about sitting in the Stadium end zone on a slushy day in November of 1972, my feet gradually freezing in my P. F. Flyers, and watching a couple of students carrying a banner, protesting the Kent State and Jackson State killings, along the edge of the brick wall separating the stands from the field. "Stop Racist Murder in Amerika" it read, and I couldn't understand the misspelling.

And standing in a pouring rain outside the Stadium at halftime of the 2007 OSU game, which Michigan was losing and would lose, badly, and staring at the immense unhappy crowd milling about, and yet somehow suddenly having a Proustian sense that I would remember this moment with nothing but fondness many years later, and now I do. And the last Michigan game I attended before the pandemic, sitting next to a six-year-old boy at his very first Michigan game, and wondering if one day he too would find himself entangled in memories of the irrecoverable past.

"The great thing," a writer once wrote, "is to last and get your work done and see and hear and learn and understand; and write when there is something that you know; and not before; and not too damned much after."

We're captive on the carousel of time.

ACKNOWLEDGMENTS

All books are to some extent collective efforts; this one is very much the work of many contributors, who helped in various ways to bring it into being.

My brother Isaac Campos first suggested to me that, in his words, fandom is folly. Our many discussions of that idea provided the original basis for this project. He also read and provided a detailed critique of the book's first draft, which helped shaped its ultimate form.

Michael Elkon also read the original draft of the book's manuscript and provided detailed and invaluable feedback. His early support for the project meant a great deal.

Likewise, David Dahlstrom read the original version of the book, and his response, both sympathetic and critical, was immensely useful to me.

My editor Tim Mennel's deft and insightful edit of the manuscript played a key role in bringing it to its final form. Jenni Fry's copyedit, which she undertook under trying circumstances, tactfully saved me from a hyperbolic blunder or three.

I'm also grateful to two anonymous reviewers for the University of Chicago Press for their comments and suggestions.

My agent Susan Schulman called upon her considerable reserves of patience and tact to help turn what agents refer to as a "quirky" project—*quirky* being agent shorthand for "I don't want to represent this"—into a viable commercial entity.

My wife Jenny has gracefully endured two years of obsessing about an obsession and has contributed to the project directly via her insights as a competitive athlete, as the book's text illustrates.

Dave Bajo is a great writer, a great friend, and an exemplary Michigan fan. Our countless conversations over the years on this and many related subjects have left an indelible mark on my thinking.

Michael Thirman and Sam Silver are two other friends from my years in Ann Arbor whose cynical affection for the Wolverines and the Cornhuskers respectively provided a certain dour inspiration for this project.

I'm particularly grateful to many longtime members of the Michigan board, who each in their own way made this book what it is. Although I'm by necessity omitting dozens of names from this list, I want to thank Steve Angelotti, Randy Balamut, Jeff Burke, Jon Chait, Ed Cohen, Steve Cox, J. D. Cronin, Bob Johnston, Mike Judson, Ian Laing, Nick Mahanic, Mike Meggyesy, Vijay Ramanujan, Danny Rudolph, Brent Shull, Hank Volquardsen, Rich Walkowski, and Craig Weston.

This book is dedicated to William Ian Miller. Thirty-five years ago in Ann Arbor, Bill taught me a little about property law and a great deal more about the Icelandic blood feud. In the decades since, he has by example shown me how to pursue interesting ideas in a serious way, and vice versa. I hope this book reflects the quality of his mentorship.